A Rose from the

ASHES

THE ROSE PRICE STORY

THE ROSE PRICE STORY

Purple Pomegranate Productions
San Francisco, CA

A Rose from the Ashes. The Rose Price Story
as told to Naomi Rothstein
© 2006 by Purple Pomegranate Productions
(a division of Jews for Jesus®)
Cover design by David Yapp

For more information, including reprint permission, write to:
Jews for Jesus®
60 Haight Street
San Francisco, CA 94102
USA
www.jewsforjesus.org

ISBN 10: 1-881022-66-8
ISBN 13: 978-1-881022-66-4

CONTENTS

ACKNOWLEDGMENTS

Thank you Talbot Spivak, Stan Weinberg and all the people who helped with this book.

This book is in memory of my Momma, Poppa, my little sister, my brother, Bubbe and Zayde, the whole family, aunts, uncles and cousins, the six million who were murdered just because they are Jews.

Special acknowledgment to the memory of Rachmiel Fryland and Richard & Sabina Wurmbrandt.

FOREWORD

I first met Rose Price in the summer of 1981. I was a zealous, new Jewish believer attending the school of Business Administration at the University of Buffalo at the time. Rose was scheduled to be the guest speaker at our Messianic Fellowship, Congregation B'rith HaDoshah that coming weekend. I had volunteered to drive up to Toronto to pick her up. From the moment I met her, I absolutely fell in love with her.

Rose shared her dramatic testimony with me during the entire 90-minute drive back to Buffalo. I listened spellbound as she shared about her childhood in Poland and the day her life changed forever in 1939 when the Germans occupied her little village, the horrors she experienced in labor camps and the destruction of her entire family, save one sister.

Understandably, Rose lost her faith in God. After all, how could a God of love allow such suffering and misery? How could the God of Israel allow six million of his own people, the Children of Israel, to be brutally snuffed out? Yet for some reason, her identity as a Jew remained important to her. As she began to rebuild her life, moved to the United States, married and raised a family, she remained active in the Jewish community and synagogue life. She even became president of her synagogue. She kept a Jewish home and raised her three children as Jews.

Everything was seemingly fine . . . that is until her oldest
daughter came home one day and suddenly announced
"Mommy, I believe in Jesus Christ! He is the Jewish
Messiah!" In Rose's own words, "If she'd opened her jacket,
pulled out a gun and shot me, it would have been better
than hearing those words!"

For Rose, Jesus was not an option. Jesus and his followers
were, after all, to blame for the systematic murder of six
million Jews, including almost her entire family. The
banner she had read stretched across the entrance to
Dachau "YOU KILLED OUR GOD, JESUS CHRIST, AND
NOW, WE KILL YOU" had reinforced this in her mind.
Nazis and Christians were one and the same. To her, the
Nazis **were** Christians, doing what Jesus had commanded
them to do . . . hate the Jews.

This is the understanding of most of the mainstream Jewish
community today. There is no distinction made between a
true follower of Jesus Christ and a Gentile or a Nazi. For
Jews, Christians are to blame for a 2,000 year legacy of
hatred and anti-Semitism: The Crusaders, as they marched
through Europe and slaughtered entire Jewish communities;
the Spanish Inquisition, where some Jews were forced to
convert to Christianity by the edge of the sword and others
were burned alive; the pogroms of Eastern Europe; and
ultimately, the Holocaust were all perpetrated in the name of
Christ and Christianity. It should be no wonder that even
the name Jesus Christ is a bone in the throat of most Jews
and it was for Rose.

She was angry and confused. She didn't know what to do.
She loved her daughter yet she could not allow that
daughter to embrace the very evil that had destroyed her
family and caused her such intense suffering. So she
sought help. She went to her rabbi, met with a Catholic

seminary professor, and even began to study the Scriptures (including the New Testament) to prove her daughter was wrong about Jesus. I won't elaborate further on the incredible spiritual pilgrimage that followed since it is beautifully retold in detail in the pages that follow. Only to say that she came to an amazing discovery that transformed her life forever.

One last thought. For those of you who, like me, were raised in a Jewish home and taught that believing in Jesus (who I thought was the son of Mr. and Mrs. Christ, God of the Gentiles) is not Jewish and that it is impossibile to still be Jewish and believe in him, I want to urge you to read this book with an open heart and mind. It may just be possible that our rabbis were wrong then, when they rejected him as Messiah and are wrong today. Ask God to show you the truth and he will. He changed my life 26 years ago after I asked him to show me, he changed Rose's life 35 years ago, and he can change your life too!

Rose's story is a testimony of unimaginable suffering, heartfelt searching and ultimately restored faith and divine forgiveness. Her story is one of tragedy to triumph.

My encounter with Rose more than a quarter of a century ago changed my life and I believe that as you read her story it will change your life as well.

Jonathan Bernis
Phoenix, Arizona
March 26, 2006

PRELUDE

I was freezing. The wind howled outside the barracks as my sister Sarah and I huddled together, trying to stay warm and fall asleep at the same time. The barracks teemed with the sounds of other women snoring, crying, in some cases arguing. I was just finally feeling sleep wash over me, when suddenly the barracks door swung open and four Nazi guards marched in. "Rose! Rose Lubah!" they shouted. My body stiffened with fear. "Why are they looking for me?" I whispered to Sarah. She didn't answer. I guessed that she was asleep. How could she sleep through the noise, I wondered. I could hear the guards coming closer to my bunk, the hollow clomp of their boots on the floor. Then, the footsteps stopped. I lay in the bunk, trying to breathe, hoping they would pass by. "Rose!" the guard screamed. Startled, I exhaled quickly and loudly. A hand grabbed my arm and pulled me off the bunk to the floor. "I found her!" the one guard shouted to the others as he began dragging me from my bunk, to the door of the barracks. "No!" I screamed, "Please, no! No!"

A hand shook me. "Rose! Rose, wake up!" As the noises of the barracks and the guards faded from my mind, I could hear my husband's voice. "Rose, shhhhh" he said gently. "It was a nightmare. You're safe. Shhhh. You're safe."

I opened my eyes and looked at him, the horror of my dream still clinging to my heart, making it beat fast. "Hold me," I told him. "Please hold me."

MY POPPA

My mind wandered back to a much earlier time. I was three years old, frustrated and confused as I sat on the hard floor of our house, trying to pull on my thick wool stockings and shoes all by myself. I had finally managed to get the stockings on, but they were all twisted, and I couldn't figure out which shoe was supposed to go on which foot.

Poppa, seated in a chair in front of me, looked down at his disconcerted little girl. Silently, he moved to join me on the floor. He pulled me into his lap and began straightening my stockings, making sure each toe was in its right place. Then he pulled my leather shoes on. As he laced them, I leaned back into his chest. I can still feel his beard on my neck and my tiny feet in his large hands. It is a recollection of pure love.

I've always associated my Poppa with feelings of comfort. One of my earliest memories of him is the time I found myself in the kitchen alone. I was about four years old. My Bubbe had left a large pot on the stove, and my nose detected the tantalizing sweet smell of marmalade. Ours was a big, wood-burning stove, twice as tall as me. From my vantage point, I could barely make out the handle of the wooden spoon sticking out of the pot. "I bet I can reach it," I thought. "Nobody will know if I just take a little taste." I stood up on my tiptoes to make myself taller. But as I reached for the spoon, I lost my balance and stumbled, knocking over the entire pot of boiling sticky liquid. It spread over my hands. Oh, how it hurt! I still have the scars. I screamed in pain until

Poppa appeared and poured cold water over my scorched fingers, and held me until I stopped crying.

Poppa was a quiet, soft-spoken man. He worked very hard as a house painter, putting in long hours from dawn until dusk. When he wasn't working and wasn't exhausted, he spent most of his time reading the Torah. He frequently told us children, "Be proud, for you are chosen of God." And when Friday night came, the beginning of Shabbat—the Sabbath—Poppa transformed into the most loving, joyful man in the world. I never hesitated to jump onto his lap and smother him with kisses. He always feigned annoyance that I "messed up" his long beard, but I knew by the twinkle in his eye that he loved it.

By far, the most haunting memory I have of my father is the first time I ever saw his feet.

I was nine years old. My sister Sarah and I came home from school to find a crowd of people in our house, and yet it was so quiet. Always curious, I pushed through the maze of family and friends to the center of the room.

Then I saw a body covered by a sheet. The feet poked out over the bed. They were shoeless. And even though I'd never laid eyes on his feet before, I knew that these were my father's toes.

I looked around frantically, trying to figure out what was going on, but no one spoke to me. I felt swamped by all the people moving slowly through the house. I looked for Momma and Bubbe, but couldn't see them.

When I began to cry, someone ushered me outside. No one mentioned the word "death." No one said, "Your Poppa is dead. He is all gone forever." Perhaps everyone thought I was too young to understand. Sarah knew, but for some reason didn't spell it out for me. She knew that an old Jewish tradition states that when someone dies, his body must face out of the room, feet first as if leaving home with bare feet to enter cleanly into heaven. As for me, I was lost.

I later found out that Poppa had suffered a heart attack,
the result of fleeing from some Polish youths who were
chasing him, threatening to beat him up. It was not
uncommon for Polish boys to harass Jewish people in this
way. Poppa ran so hard and so fast he collapsed.

In our town, as in all Jewish towns, there was an
association, the *Chevrah Kadisha*, whose duty it was to take
care of the dead. They dressed the body, and took my father
to the place where he would be buried.

I didn't understand that it was my time to grieve for
Poppa, though at the gravesite people forced me to look
down into the grave. No one told me what he was doing
there. In fact, out of kindness I'm sure, some hinted that he
would soon come back.

And so for months, I sat on the corner of my street every
day waiting for my Poppa. I thought, "Maybe God is
punishing me because I've misbehaved. If I am a good girl,
Poppa will come back."

Of course, Poppa never returned home.

I was perhaps too young an age to become so acquainted
with death, and yet, little did I know that this was only the
beginning of my sorrows—of things that no child should
ever have to endure.

Poppa died just a few years before the Nazis invaded
Poland. I've often thought that perhaps God was being kind
to him; he did not have to watch his family being destroyed.

There are still days when I miss my Poppa. And even
though the events of my life have often made me doubt, I
have never, ever forgotten his words: "Be proud, for you are
chosen of God."

PART ONE

BEFORE THE NIGHTMARE

CHAPTER ONE

SHABBAT

Baruch atah Adonai Eloheinu meleck ha olam,
asher kid'shanu bimitzvotav vitzivanu,
lichadlich ner shel shabbat.

"Blessed are you Lord our God, King of the universe,
who has sanctified us by his commandments,
and commanded us to light the Sabbath lights."

If I close my eyes, I can still see my Momma's face and eyes glowing in the light of the Shabbat candles. Around the world, Jewish women start the Shabbat this way. When I was a child, Meyer and "Third Street" in Skarzysko, Poland was my whole world. On Friday nights, if I looked out the window, I could see candles being lit in all the Jewish houses in the neighborhood. After my father died, Momma, my sisters Sarah and Esther, my brother Nathan and I all moved into one room in my grandparents' house. It was crowded, but it was good to be together. Of course there was no Social Security or Medicare in those days. Family cared for family. It was now Momma's job to raise us.

Up until that point, we'd lived a fairly carefree childhood. But things soon changed. "You must behave even better now," Momma told us. "Bubbe and Zayde are family, but this is no longer our house."

"Will we still have Shabbat?" I asked.

"Of course," Momma replied. "It will just be different that's all."

I sighed with relief. As Orthodox Jews, Shabbat was the highlight of our week. The long days of work and school ended happily in a celebration every Friday night. But above all, Shabbat was to be holy, and so preparations began much earlier in the week.

On Wednesdays, Momma sent me to the butcher for the chicken that was slaughtered ritually. Ritual slaughter meant that the blood was drained from the animal and prayers were said over it. On Thursdays, Momma baked the cakes and the *challah* bread. On Fridays, we children cleaned up the house.

Sometimes we held Friday night Shabbat dinner in our own room at the back of Zayde's house, partly because Momma thought we kids made too much noise for Bubbe's front room Shabbat dinner. But we often celebrated there too.

Zayde's house served as the synagogue for our family and friends. Zayde's work was designing and fashioning shoe tops and his workshop was in the house. But every Friday afternoon, Zayde closed down his business so the large room in the center of the house could be prepared for worship. The sewing machines were carried away and the Ark that held the sacred Torah scrolls was wheeled out. It was actually a wooden cabinet that stood in a corner the rest of the week, but on Shabbat it was the Ark of the Covenant. Then, after Zayde changed his clothes and washed his hands, he would walk around the room clapping and singing songs to the Lord in his deep, mellow voice.

Meanwhile the women—Bubbe and Momma, and perhaps an aunt—kept busy in the kitchen making last minute preparations for the Shabbat meal, which had to be ready before sundown because no work could take place after that. Steam rose from large metal pots, like a savory-smelling invitation to a special evening.

The meal itself was nothing elaborate, but always included fresh baked *challah* bread, some fish, chicken soup with noodles, and most of the time, pieces of chicken. Gefilte fish (white fish or pike, ground up, mixed with bread or matzah, and shaped into oblong patties) served cold with horseradish, often accompanied the meal. We finished with apple or sponge cake.

The table was made of rough hardwood; it wasn't polished or stained. We scrubbed it down with brushes and soap. After it dried we spread a simple, crocheted cotton tablecloth over it. The candlesticks we used were made of brass and silver, and they had a simple geometric flower design etched in them. They were shined every week, and when we set them on the table along with our dishes and napkins, the whole room took on a beauty that seemed reserved for this one day of the week.

Dishes of course, were important. Our household had four sets of dishes. Each person had his or her own plate, cup and utensils. Two sets were reserved just for Passover and the third set for Shabbat. Our everyday dishes were kept in a separate cupboard and when the meal was served, we took what was necessary. We had extra settings for guests.

Often twelve to fifteen people, not always the same, came to Shabbat dinner. There was Bubbe, Zayde, Momma, we four children, and Rose, my mother's younger sister, who wasn't married. Aunt Rose was a librarian and she always carried a book under her arm. Her books and her profession commanded a certain respect. We behaved accordingly, especially when Aunt Rose went off into a corner by herself to read. Often, someone from the synagogue or a stranger in town was also invited to Shabbat dinner.

Everyone greeted each other with warmth and enthusiasm, but the chatter subsided as the last rays of sunlight slipped away and we began the meal. Covering her head with a shawl, Bubbe or Momma lit two candles and said the prayers ushering in Shabbat. Zayde blessed the wine and the bread. All these prayers were in praise of God. They began, "Blessed are you, Lord our God, Ruler of the Universe."

The meal itself was festive. Any concerns of the past week seemed to grow pale in the glory of the Shabbat. Laughter often rippled up and down the table. Wisdom seemed to flow from the mouths of elders. Children's voices, while not entirely muted, did not predominate.

After dinner, we cleared the dishes away and prepared to pray. The men in the room all wore *kippot* (skullcaps). As Orthodox Judaism dictates, the women gathered apart from the men. We congregated in the kitchen, behind drawn drapes. I wonder to this day what the men discussed when they weren't praying. Even my cousin Abraham wouldn't tell me, though I threatened him with bodily harm.

While the men were praying in the living room, Bubbe gathered the children in the kitchen and told us about the wonderful heroes of the *Tanakh*. Every Friday night, I went to bed with my mind full of tales of heroism, virtue and faith. As the Sabbath prayers and the flames of the Shabbat candles rose to God, I glowed with the knowledge that the next day would also be filled with joy and praise in the cradle of my family.

On Saturday mornings, we girls put on our best dresses. In summer our best dresses were made of cotton, in winter they were made of wool. Some years our dresses had flower designs or mixed colors, and sometime they were plain. In both summer and winter, our dresses fell to the knees and had long sleeves. Under them we wore one-piece slips— *gatkes* we called them—which buttoned up the rear. Modesty was essential.

After a simple breakfast of a piece of *challah* and a glass of tea or milk, we set off to synagogue on foot. Orthodox Jews cannot carry anything on Shabbat except the key to the house. Our house key was secured to Zayde's wrist with a handkerchief. Since kids less than thirteen were allowed to carry things, I was elected to carry the prayer books for

Zayde, Bubbe, Momma and any other adult with us. Week
after week, they piled their books on my arms, so high I
sometimes couldn't see where I was going. It got to be too
much. One Saturday morning, I crossed the street and
stacked the books on the windowsill of a store, all except
those of my immediate family. It was my way of saying, "Just
because I'm the smallest doesn't mean you can make me do
whatever you want." From then on, no one asked me to
carry his or her books. Zayde understood and wasn't mad.

The synagogue was a handsome red brick building, built by
the city with contributions from the Jewish community. The
Ark, of carved and polished wood, was set in the eastern wall.
The bima (podium), stood in the middle of the room. It was
large—at least six feet wide by three feet deep—big enough
to hold the Torah scroll when it was unrolled to be read. It
was set on a platform with an iron railing around it. Men
were called up from the congregation to read. They all looked
so dignified in their *tallesim* (prayer shawls). The synagogue
was beautifully furnished; even the wooden benches were
comfortable. The women always sat upstairs in the balcony.
"Are we closer to God up here?" I sometimes wondered.

Walking home from synagogue, we looked forward to the
afternoon dinner. The leftovers from the night before would
taste even better. Bubbe and Momma purposely made
enough on Friday for our Saturday afternoon meal. But we
didn't rely only on leftovers. The morning before, Momma
and Bubbe prepared a huge pot of meat and vegetables. On
Saturday, I carried the large pot to the bakery. Other families
did the same; the bakery had an oven large enough to heat
such pots. They had baked their breads for the day, but the
ovens were still hot, so for a few *kopeks* our food was
cooked for us so we wouldn't have to break the Sabbath's
prohibition against work.

After dinner, Zayde rose from the table to go take his
afternoon nap. He was the father of our whole family; it was
his day of rest. Oh how quiet we were then! When Zayde

woke up, he sat all the children at a long table, in order according to our ages. We got our Bibles out and he taught us about God. He considered this his most important job. We had better know our lessons, or God forbid, a disappointed look would spread over his face. He was stern, but gentle. His questions would come slowly then. "You did not learn? You don't know what that means?" Punishment began and ended with his disappointment. His high expectations were his way of showing us his love.

Bubbe also gathered us around her so she could read the Bible to us. God's love was the theme of much of her teaching. She often read the Joseph story, from which she taught us, "Children, remember, you must look out for each other, not take advantage of each other like Joseph's brothers. You are each other's keepers. And you older ones, especially, must look out for the younger."

And that was Shabbat. We did nothing but read Scripture. As the sun began to set, we all wished we could hold onto the daylight just a bit more; it was wonderful to linger in the grace of God's special day. At last we could delay Zayde no longer. He put out the candles for the *Havdalah* service. Bubbe or Momma, or maybe one of my aunts, cut up a cake. I still remember the delightful sugary smell of the sponge or pound cake. Though it had been baked several days before, it was as fresh as ever.

Shabbat was over, and work began again. Everyone helped put away the ceremonial items. "Rose, come do the dishes," Momma often said, and I would. As I washed them, I sometimes daydreamed of being permitted to snuff out the candles, though I knew that only Zayde or my cousin Abraham was allowed to do that.

I never imagined that a time was coming soon when Zayde and Abraham would be no more. I never imagined that the plates and saucers I washed with such care would all be smashed to pieces, or stolen to serve another family who wouldn't even understand why we had so many sets of dishes.

CHAPTER TWO

LIFE IN SKARZYSKO

Living with Bubbe and Zayde meant that our days were usually very busy. It seemed the house was always full of people. I frequently opened the door to women looking for "Riva Schpits", my Bubbe, who was affectionately called that because she was "very wise, very smart." Everyone came to her for answers to their problems, sometimes from the other side of the city. They huddled with Bubbe, crying and whispering desperately about husbands or children or finances. She listened, touching their shoulders lightly sometimes, offering advice. The women drank the tea and ate the buttered bread Bubbe served them and went away comforted. She was the angel of our neighborhood.

The big room in the center of the house was Zayde's workshop, where he designed and created custom-fitted shoe tops. "Come here," he said to me one day, and motioned me toward him with his finger. I stood at his side and watched as he cut the leather by hand with a special knife and fashioned flowers, mountains and spirals into the points of the shoes. It was such intricate and captivating work. With large machines he sewed the tops to the sides, front and back of each shoe. "Zayde, can I run one of the machines today?" I asked. He shook his head, "No." (My

Zayde was a wise man.) That was a job for my aunts and uncles. "But do you think you can hold this shoe top nice and steady for me?" he asked. I nodded yes. Then he let me put the tops of the shoes on a form while he hammered them. I beamed with pride—I was helping! I so badly wanted to please my Zayde.

One spring day, around Passover, I was running barefoot along a trail in the woods behind our house. Suddenly I felt a searing pain in my foot. I had stepped on something sharp, cutting my foot deeply. The blood began staining the brown leaves left over from winter. I screamed and Zayde came rushing from the house.

"What have you done?" he cried and seeing my foot, he scooped me up quickly and carried me inside. "How could you be so careless," he scolded me after he'd treated the wound. "With such a deep cut, you could get a serious infection, or blood poisoning, or even gangrene!"

I sensed his anger toward me and his disappointment, which hurt me far worse than the cut on my foot. But I also felt his love for me in those moments, which reminded me of my father's love for me, and I vowed never to make him angry with me again. "I'm sorry, Zayde," I said.

"Besides," Bubbe interjected, her eyes sparkling, "If you hurt your foot then who will help me make preserves?"

I smiled. I so looked forward to harvest time. Through the spring and summer, we weeded and watered little vegetable patches, but when it came time to harvest, the real fun began. Practically everything we grew was preserved in one way or another. The vegetables had to be compressed as tightly as possible to last all winter. So Zayde prepared large wooden barrels to store the food, while Bubbe put fresh white stockings on our feet. Then Zayde lifted us into the barrels to keep our feet from touching the floor. Our job was to jump and bounce on the vegetables, especially the cabbages, to squash them together.

I still remember how fun it was to jump with all my might on those vegetables. When we squashed the vegetables down below the rim, they dumped more in and we jumped and bounced some more. At last, when the barrels were brimming full to the rim, Zayde lifted us out and Bubbe stretched a tight cloth over the barrels and nailed wooden covers to the tops. Then the men rolled the barrels down into the basement where it was always cool, so the food stayed well preserved. The basement floor was hard packed earth, so we buried potatoes in the dirt to keep them from spoiling. Beets too. Nothing was thrown out. We used everything. We also took turns at the churn, making butter and cheese. Who needed a supermarket?

Bubbe was also knowledgeable about the use of plants and herbs. If one of us caught a cold or cough, she boiled onions and sugar to make a cough medicine. One spoonful cured everything, it seemed. She frequently sent us foraging in the forest to collect mushrooms, berries and specific green leaves. With these she prepared an ointment for burns. When I spilled the hot marmalade over my hands, that ointment saved my skin from peeling off.

One day, I noticed a smudge of something behind Bubbe's ear. When I asked her what it was, she replied, "It's a leech."

"But why don't you pry it off?"

"Leeches help your Bubbe with her high blood pressure," she responded. "Now have you milked the goats yet today?"

I grabbed the pail and headed outside to the fenced area in the backyard where we kept the goats so they wouldn't munch on our vegetables. They shared the grassy area with our chickens. As I passed the chickens, I couldn't help but shudder thinking of my own poor pet.

We raised chickens in our backyard, and always had fresh eggs. Each of us children claimed one of the chickens as our own pet. Oh, how we cared for them! But Momma warned us not to grow too attached. I couldn't understand why until the day I saw my chicken strung up by the *Shoychet* (ritual slaughterer).

"You killed my chicken!" I cried. "How could you kill my chicken?"

"Rose," my mother responded, "How else do you think we get chickens for Shabbat dinner? I warned you not to get too attached."

That night, I, Rose, who was born hungry, lost my appetite. I left the table when my chicken was brought out in a steaming pot. From then on, the chickens and I were no longer friendly. So that afternoon, I merely stepped past them and over them as I chased the goats around with a pail in one hand and a stool in the other.

The goats' milk was for my sister Sarah. She was two years older than I, but was a sickly little girl. When she was eight years old, she developed a condition we called "water in the belly." To this day, I don't know what it was, but Poppa had to take her to a big city hospital to "tap out the water." That's when Bubbe decided Sarah needed goats' milk. When I got to be about seven or eight years old, milking the goats became my job, and I did it willingly. It was one of my many chores.

Our days and lives had a steady, dependable routine to them. Every day we woke up, washed, said our morning prayers, got dressed, prayed again, had breakfast, went to school, returned and had a snack. Then we went to the *cheder* (Hebrew school) to learn Hebrew. By the time we returned home it was almost dark. We did our homework, had dinner and completed our share of housework. Also the chickens, geese and goats had to be fed and cleaned. We went to bed very tired, and fell asleep quickly. We never had time to be bored.

I suppose we were poor, but everyone in our neighborhood was in the same situation, so if we were poor, we didn't know it. We had lots of friends. Our aunts and uncles lived only a few doors away. If it started to rain while we were playing, we could always run into their houses to be greeted with milk and cookies and love.

Of all my uncles and aunts, my absolute favorite was Uncle Meyer. He was so kind. He always made time for us, listening attentively to our questions and taking us seriously. He often wore a tie and striped shirt. He never wore the old-fashioned black hats. Uncle Meyer sported a modern felt hat, the kind seen in America from the 1930s through the 1950s. To me, he was just the perfect man. Nobody made time for me like he did.

And then one day he came over to the house with a woman and said, "This is Lubah and we are going to be married." I was almost ten years old at the time; he must have been in his early twenties. I couldn't believe my ears. I stood there, jaw open, and my eyes must have been shooting daggers at them both, because Uncle Meyer quickly asked, "What's wrong, Rose?" I couldn't articulate it then, but immediately I hated this Lubah, this stranger who was stealing my Uncle Meyer away from me.

Of course, Uncle Meyer couldn't understand why I was so upset, why I could never warm up to his fiancé. He treated me as kindly as ever; my jealousy was a mystery to him. And of course, that hurt even more.

"Sarah, hold still!"

"What are you doing, Rose, stop it!"

I had in my hand a fresh egg from a chicken, still warm, and I was trying to hold it to Sarah's eyes. Bubbe and Momma did this sometimes; it was supposed to be good for us somehow. But Sarah was unwilling to cooperate with me while I tried to play the adult.

"Sarah, just close your eyes; I'm not going to hurt you." Finally, she acquiesced. I held the warm egg to her eye and began to rub it lightly over her eyelids—but apparently not lightly enough, because suddenly it broke and Sarah's face was covered in egg yolk. She cried out and Bubbe and Momma came rushing into the room.

"What's wrong with you?" my mother shouted.

I got a good beating for that incident. Sarah's fragility made her Momma's favorite, and it seemed like I was always getting blamed for things. I got pegged as the rebellious one, and to a certain extent, rightly so. After my father died, I became more insolent and stubborn.

Back then, the only answer was discipline. I was spanked; I was slapped. It didn't matter; I didn't care. Sarah marveled at how I could shake off a reprimand or a punishment. Her face would burn for hours where Momma had given her a slight smack that for me would have been equal to a caress. Her feelings were bruised by one of Bubbe's gentle reminders that I forgot by the time Bubbe had uttered it.

Looking back, I wonder if perhaps this was God's way of preparing me. I would soon need to become a very tough girl in order to protect both my Sarah and myself.

CHAPTER THREE

FROM PASSOVER TO PURIM

It was spring—almost time for Passover! There was so much to do. Every time I turned around Momma or Bubbe were asking me to do something. The house had to be scrubbed from top to bottom, and any speck of leaven had to be removed before the eight-day Feast of Unleavened Bread.

Searching for the leaven was kind of a game for us. After the first room was completely cleaned, no one was allowed in it. Then we washed the special Passover dishes and cooking utensils in boiling water and someone brought everything into that one clean room, to store it there until it was time to celebrate. Then we marched on, relentlessly cleaning and ferreting out all traces of leaven in the rest of the house. This physical cleaning had its spiritual analogue in the cleansing of our souls, but we children didn't think this through at the time.

My most important and favorite Pesach job though, was to help prepare the matzah, the unleavened bread of affliction that the Israelites baked in haste when they left Egypt. We needed lots of matzah, not only for the Seder meal, but because we weren't allowed to eat any leavened bread for eight days.

Zayde made the matzah at the bakery. I always helped him roll the flour. Other men from the synagogue joined in. We rolled the dough flat as we could, then made tiny holes in it with a special smaller roller. This thin, fragile dough was then placed in the large open ovens for a few minutes until it was time to turn it over. The men always teased me because I wasn't big enough to flip the matzah with the four-foot-long wooden "spatula." So I became the watcher, the "*shoymera*." When I didn't pay close attention, the men yelled at me because even thirty seconds too long in those ovens would burn the matzah to a crisp. Zayde would then threaten me with a rolling pin, which he wouldn't dream of using. I remember once I cried all the way home because I had let some of the matzah burn.

Besides the matzah, there were so many other dishes to prepare for the Seder meal. The Seder plate had to contain *charoset* (a sweet mixture of chopped apples, nuts, wine, honey or sugar and spices) and *maror* (bitter herbs of ground horseradish or romaine lettuce), which all had to be prepared in advance.

All of the effort was worth it. I looked forward to Passover all winter. As the feast of freedom, it commemorates the story of the Exodus when we were liberated from bondage in Egypt. Every Passover we retell the story of how God redeemed the Israelites after four hundred years of slavery. "We were slaves to Pharaoh . . ." begins the account.

We remember the pain and degradation of the whip. We understand fear and hopelessness—our own and others'. We remember the stranger because we were once strangers in a strange land. The Exodus, and thus Passover, is central in Jewish thought and prayer.

To this day, I can still hear the Four Questions that the youngest child who can read chants near the beginning of the Seder. *Ma nishtanah halailah hazeh mikol haleylos?* begins the series of questions and answers. "Why is this night

different from all other nights? Why do we eat only
unleavened bread, matzah? Why do we eat only bitter herbs?
Why do we dip our vegetables twice? Why do we eat
reclining?"

It is a night when children are encouraged to ask
questions, and it is a duty and privilege during the Seder to
answer these questions and to retell the story of God's
mighty acts and his redemptive faithfulness.

And then came one of my favorite parts. "Alright, children,"
Zayde said, his brown eyes shining. "It's time." With those
words, all the children scattered, looking for the afikomen.

During the seder, three pieces of matzah are placed in a
pouch. Towards the beginning of the meal, as part of the set
order of service, the middle piece of matzah is broken in half.
One half is placed back in the pouch. The other is wrapped
in cloth and hidden from sight, while all the children cover
their eyes. Later, the "search for the afikomen" commences,
and the one child who finds it has to give it back to the head
of the household, and then he or she is usually rewarded.

When I was a child, the seder meal seemed to last forever.
I doubt I ever made it past the soup and matzah balls before
falling asleep. I always woke up in my bed, the sweet taste
of raisin wine still on my tongue.

Zayde's raisin wine was the sweetest, most delicious wine in
the world. Every year, he took a basket of dried grapes and cut
them into pieces. Actually, he allowed my sisters and me to cut
them up, but he had to watch me very closely. I cheated a lot.
For every five raisins I chopped, one was stuffed into my
mouth. When we were done, Zayde put the pieces into a five-
gallon glass jug, and pressed them down so they would
ferment into the delectable juice we drank at Passover.

Passover is part of a holiday cycle that gives our lives a
rhythm; a reliable sequence of commemorations. From the

second night of Passover, we count the Omer, the fifty days to Shavuot. Originally, the Omer was the first offering, or measure, of the new grain harvest brought to the Temple. The Torah doesn't tell us why this is important, but over the years it has come to be associated with marking the days until the Torah was revealed at Mount Sinai.

Shavuot celebrates God's gift of the Torah to the Jewish people. Though the Bible doesn't specifically state this, after the destruction of the Temple in 70 A.D., rabbis began to make the connection between the revelation at Sinai and Shavuot. The Book of Ruth is usually read during this holiday—her voluntary conversion to Judaism is analogous to our acceptance of God's covenant at Sinai. This Covenant, finally and forever sealed, provides a basis for the Jewish religion. Shavuot is also seen as the marriage between God and Israel, his bride.

The summer months after Shavuot mark a series of tragedies that have befallen the Jewish people. The first and second temples were both destroyed on the ninth of Av. With the destruction of the second temple, Jewish sovereignty over Jerusalem ended, and the great Diaspora (dispersion) and exile began. This period of mourning begins in fasting and ends with the fast of *Tisha b'Av*.

In the fall, Rosh Hashanah begins the High Holidays and the New Year. The *shofar*, or ram's horn is blown, perhaps to awaken us, perhaps as a cry and lament of the people of Israel down through the ages. This commences a time when we examine our lives and our actions of the past year and ask for forgiveness for what we have done wrong in God's eyes. Yet, asking is not enough. We must be truly contrite, feel remorse for the harm we have done, and strive for atonement. If we have hurt others we must ask them for forgiveness. We greet one another, *Le'shanah tovah tikatevu."* May you be inscribed in the Book of Life for a good year."

After ten days of repentance comes Yom Kippur, a day of atonement, when our very existence, as it were, hangs in the balance. We enter Yom Kippur chanting Kol Nidre, proclaiming those promises and vows that we make—but do not keep in the New Year—null and void. Aware that we are not perfect, we ask God *in advance* to forgive us for our failings. In the Sephardic tradition, we ask that unfulfilled vows of the past year be forgiven. Periodically throughout the evening and the next day, lists of sins are recited. The extraordinary power of these recitations ends with our asking God to forgive us. We fast from sundown to sundown. During Yom Kippur we must turn toward God, or return to God. Prayer alone is not enough; we must change our behavior toward our fellow human beings.

Five days following this period of repentance, there is a time of great joy called Sukkot, a harvest festival. It was during Sukkot that Solomon consecrated the Temple. We build a small-framed structure open to the sky and winds, decorating it for this agricultural festival with hanging gourds and fruit. Families eat (and some even sleep) in their sukkah. It is a temporary structure to remind us of those our ancestors the Israelites erected and took down as they wandered forty years in the desert.

As Sukkot, or the Feast of Tabernacles, comes to a close, it anticipates Zechariah's words that one day, "everyone remaining from all the nations that came to attack Jerusalem will go up every year to worship the King, the Lord of Hosts, and to keep the festival of Sukkot."

The Bible asks us to dwell one more day with the Lord after the seven days of Sukkot: Shemini Atzeret. It is also associated with prayers for rain during the winter months. About a thousand years ago, rabbis began to celebrate the completion of the yearlong cycle of reading the Torah on the second day, Simchat Torah, the joy of Torah as it was carried around the synagogue. Each man would pass it off to the next, who would receive the sacred weight of the scrolls blissfully, in joyful awe that he was carrying the word of God.

Hanukkah, in December, celebrates a miracle of light. In many Jewish homes, candles are placed in a menorah, a nine-branched candleholder. The first night one candle is lit, the second two, and so on. The youngest child lights the *shammash*, the helper candle, and with it the others. Hanukkah celebrates freedom and life, and the courage and faith of a small band of Jews in their long fight and victory over the Seleucid dynasty of hellenized Syrians. In rededicating the Temple, the Maccabees (the family that began the revolt) discovered only enough oil to light the Menorah used in Temple services to last for a day. In faith they lit it, and it stayed lit for eight days.

During Hanukkah, we sing songs, play games and give gifts. As children we loved it. So did my children and grandchildren. When I light the candles, I inwardly celebrate a personal miracle, renewed every year I am alive.

We children looked forward with great expectation to Purim, almost overlooking Tu B'Shvat. One plants things for Tu B'Shvat, as a way to help in some small way to "repair the world." But in January, planting a tree in Poland is not very practical. Deuteronomy holds that five fruits and two grains should be eaten, but again all of those five fruits rarely showed up together on our table.

Purim came a month later, and though it was not usually too much warmer in Poland, we thought of it as a harbinger of spring. We read and acted out the Book of Esther. When the name of Haman (who wanted to destroy the Jews) was read, we hooted and shook our noisemakers, blotting him out from our memory. We cheered the names of our heroes: Esther, the Jewish queen of a pagan King Ahasuerus and her uncle Mordechai, who contrived to foil Haman's plans.

During the Purim festival, joy and fun are encouraged. Dramatic skits are performed. And yet, at the center of this holiday is the fact that Haman planned to annihilate the Jewish people. He wished to exterminate us all. He marshaled the strength and collusion of many. And his plan almost succeeded.

But in the bosom of my family, we didn't fear Haman. Conscious that we were the chosen people to whom God had given his Torah, we children tasted a few drops of Zayde's wine, ate the prune-filled pastries that Bubbe and Momma made, laughed and clapped, and shared our innocent joy. Little did we realize that there was a man who intended to re-enact Haman's plot even in our time. Never did we guess, as we gathered together as a family that the recipe for Zayde's raisin wine would perish with him at an extermination camp at Treblinka.

CHAPTER FOUR

WHY DO THEY HATE US?

As I recall memories of my family celebrating the feasts of the Lord, I am jolted by moments of pain. As much as I'd like to paint a picture of an idyllic childhood, I must confront the truth: hatred and anti-Semitism often forced their way through the walls of the honeycomb of my family. I have mentioned that Passover was one of my favorite times of the year, and yet one Passover memory stands out so clearly as being one of the most horrible moments of my childhood.

I couldn't have been much more than three or four years old. One of our neighbors was a tall and muscular woman with a loud voice. She was not Jewish. One afternoon she approached me, towering over my tiny frame.

"Here, I brought you this," she said, smiling, holding out a piece of cake. The cake looked good, and it smelled as if it had just come out of the oven. My mouth began to water.

Then I remembered my mother's strict instruction: "Never eat anything a stranger gives you. Never."

I hesitated for a moment, but then my little hand went out, my body moved forward. I looked up into the face of this woman. It was no longer smiling. "Take it. Eat it!" she insisted. Still I was tentative. "I'll smack you if you don't," she threatened. And I was suddenly scared.

I took the piece of cake and had just barely bit into it when my mother came running from the house, screaming, "Stop!" She slapped my hand, knocking the cake from my little fist onto the ground. Then she gave me a slap I'd remember for years to come. The large woman had begun to laugh, her frame rolling back and forth with her laughter, and when my mother smacked me, the woman began to cackle even harder.

"A Jew hitting a Jew! And on *Pesach*!" she added, mockingly using the Jewish word for Passover.

And then shame burned in my face. Even at such a young age I knew that for the eight days of Pesach we ate no bread or cake, nothing with yeast. I stood outside our front door crying, remembering how before Pesach began, my mother, sister and I had hunted for all crumbs to make our house leaven-free.

And now I had eaten cake on Pesach! I had also eaten pork though I didn't know it; the cake was made with lard. But the woman knew. She laughed triumphantly, turned, and went back into her house, highly amused at the trick she'd played on the little Jewish girl next door.

If only that had been the solitary episode of blatant anti-Semitism I'd encounter. But such was not the case. Every day, after public school we came home for a snack, and then went to Hebrew school. On the way to Hebrew school, we had to cross a bridge that spanned railroad tracks. This bridge marked a boundary that defined our mostly-Jewish and mostly-safe neighborhood. Often on our way to Hebrew school, a crowd of Polish children and adults crowded onto the far side of the bridge, creating a barricade through which we Jewish kids had to pass. They pelted us with stones and cursed us as we ran away as fast as we could. I often came home with blood on my face or a torn blouse. If a child fought back instead of running, they would beat him, and might even pick him up, and throw him over the bridge.

One day, I made the mistake of walking on a sidewalk that went past a Catholic church. Suddenly a priest, whom I later described as "a man in a long black dress" rushed down the church steps, yelling at me. When he came level with me, he knocked me down, and grasping the heavy cross around his neck, began hitting me with it. "Christ killer!" he shouted. "Christ killer!" Finally I managed to escape his blows, and ran. Through my tears and pain, I wondered, "Who is this Christ? What had I ever done to him that I should be treated like this?"

These occurrences were nothing compared to the betrayal we would eventually suffer at the hands of our fellow Poles. With the coming of the Nazis, persecution became more organized, efficient, methodical and terrible. Our neighbors viciously attacked us. And they marched through the streets with the Gestapo, pointing out every house where a Jew lived. The reward was substantial. They were given possession of our homes, our land, our valuables.

Reason tells me that not all Polish people hated Jews. Somewhere in that city of 25,000, some must have felt pity, brotherly love, Christian compassion, human solidarity. But I never met such a person. Yet, even as I grew more and more aware of the hatred people harbored against us simply for being Jewish, I still remembered and clung to Poppa's words: "Be proud, for you are chosen of God."

PART TWO

THE BEGINNING
OF THE WAR

CHAPTER FIVE

INVASION

I began to see them everywhere. They seemed to be multiplying daily; the number of Jews coming into our city from Germany. They came in droves from all over the country. They weren't like the Jews I knew. They walked with their heads uncovered, and they wore fashionable city clothes. I thought they were snobs. Though they seemed to look down on us, I think they tried to warn us that things were changing for the worse. But even though we believed there was an evil growing in Germany, we all thought of Poland as a safe haven.

Even when we heard Poland had been invaded, I still felt relatively secure. That any force could overcome the great city of Warsaw was inconceivable to my young mind. Warsaw embodied for me an impenetrable, invincible grandeur. "Surely they cannot defeat Warsaw," I thought.

Then bombs started dropping on our town. We assumed it was because of the railroad hub. My mind recalls circumstances at that time in snapshots—German bombers passing overhead, a Polish soldier standing in the street with a rifle, shooting up at the planes, the frightened faces of friends and family.

My family and I moved to the small village of Shidlowska. That village was only a couple of streets long, but we had relatives there, and we decided to stay with them until the bombing was over.

Eight days. It took just over a week for the Nazis to
conquer our country. Upon hearing the news of German
victory, we returned home. We didn't know what else to do.
I remember that when we returned to our house, a large
black cat greeted us, rubbing against our legs, and jumping
all over us. I'm not superstitious, but the sight of that cat
made me uneasy, and I have never liked cats since.

The Nazis occupied our town on September 15, 1939. I
was eleven-years-old. And for a brief time, things seemed
normal. We settled back into life, which for me meant
school. We all seemed to exhale a collective sigh of relief.
Things were not as bad as we'd feared.

We children overheard the adults talking about how
much better things would be now that the Germans were
here. "We won't suffer as much as we did under the Poles," I
heard an older person say to Momma while we were at the
store. Another woman chimed in, "That's right. Think how
the Germans took care of the Jewish people during the
Great War." I wanted so badly to believe as they did, and so I
convinced myself that occupation wouldn't be so bad, and
that in fact, things might even improve.

Then one day at school, our lesson was suddenly
interrupted by a group of German officers. They strode into
the classroom and motioned for our teacher to stop
speaking. Then one of them murmured something to her,
which we could not hear. Suddenly she faced the class and
shouted, "If you are Jewish, come to the front!"

I looked around, startled, and the other Jewish children
and I made our way to the front of the classroom as quickly
as we could in such confusion. Then she yelled, "You Jews,
go home. You are ordered to leave this school and not come
back! We don't want you here!"

I stared at her in disbelief. This was my teacher; I had
always thought she liked me! But now her eyes were filled
with venom. I couldn't understand. Why were we being
punished? Many of us were good students—well behaved

and always trying our best. The hate that radiated from her face was so severe, I suddenly realized we were the enemy. But what I remember most was the adoring gaze she cast upon the German officer as he herded us through the door. We stood silently in the hall while other Jewish children, exiled from other classes, joined us.

Outside the school, there were adults waiting for us. They began throwing stones and cursing us. "Dirty Jews!" they screamed. Hearing the noise, the Polish children swarmed out of the school and began to hit us. Nobody stopped them. I looked around; these were fellow townspeople. These were people I knew and thought I liked. These were my classmates. I became livid. "Who do you think you are!?" I screamed in fear and anger. I felt rage come over me, and I picked up some stones and hurled them back at these traitors. But there were ten of them to each one of us. And so I ran home as fast as I could.

My mother shrieked at the sight of me. I was covered in dirt and blood and my whole body ached. "Oh my Rose!" She just held me and cried. It was beyond her comprehension that someone could do this to her child, and that others could just stand by and let it happen.

One day shortly thereafter, I was busy studying at home when I heard the door open. An eerie silence followed. I looked up and there was Zayde with his thick scarf covering his face. He stood there motionless in the middle of the room. His clothes were torn. Bubbe went to him, and without a word she gently pulled the scarf away. His chin was covered in blood and purple with bruises. Some soldiers had grabbed him and ripped out his beard.

Bubbe helped Zayde take off his coat. He was so ashamed that he turned, trying to shield us from the awful damage done to him. I cried as my Bubbe cleaned his face and neck, and the collar of his shirt. "Not my Zayde," I kept saying. I'd have rather endured many more blows at school than have had to see my grandfather so humiliated and hurt.

This was the first time that I fully realized that they
hated us just for being Jews, and that they'd hated us all
along. It didn't make any sense to me—unless . . . unless we
really were different. Unless there was something wrong
with us. "No," I told myself sharply, "We do not deserve this.
We don't."

We now know that in some towns, the Jewish residents
were slaughtered by the Polish people, not the Germans.
Their revulsion for us had simmered for years, and when the
Nazis invaded, it boiled over. The best part for them and the
worst for us, is that now they could feel justified. After all,
the people in charge hated us, too. There was nowhere for
us to go. Nowhere to feel safe.

CHAPTER SIX

HOMELESS

One day our house was ours, and the next day it wasn't. One day I had a bed and clothes and pictures and then suddenly I didn't. One day there was a place where I felt relatively safe, and the next day there was no such refuge. It was taken from us and given to someone else. And it all happened so quickly.

"Jews! Out!" screamed the Nazi soldiers as they forced their way in the door. We stared at them in disbelief, until they pointed at us with their guns. Out in the streets, Poles watched and jeered, as if it were a play being performed for their amusement. I so hated them at that moment, perhaps even more than I hated the men evicting us.

"Take only what you can carry! Hurry! Now! Out!" shouted the German officer.

Bubbe and Zayde were the first to start packing and both were crying. I couldn't believe it. Was it possible? Bubbe and Zayde crying? Zayde was the head of our community; I had never seen him so shaken. And my grandmother was the wisest woman in town. Didn't she have an answer?

I rushed to our room at the back of the house and found Momma. She was crying too as she took a big sheet, put all the bedding in it, and tied the ends together. I stood watching her. She saw me and without pausing her activity, she said, "Don't just stand there, Rose. Grab something. We have to hurry." Just as she'd spoken those words, the Nazis burst into the room, shouting orders to get out.

39

Our family huddled in the street with the few belongings we'd been able to drag out of the house. Then, with other Jews who had been ordered from their homes, we were herded into an area of town no more than a street and a half in length, and a few blocks wide. Guards formed a barricade around this small area. "Welcome to your new home," one of them sneered.

"Momma, how can we all fit in just a few blocks? There aren't homes for all of us!"

It was up to everyone to carve out places for themselves in the ghetto. Momma, Sarah, Esther, Nathan and I wound up in a yard formerly used for horses. The stalls were divided into tiny enclosures. We packed into one so tightly that if the door had opened inwards instead of out, one of us might have been crushed. There was no heat. Even in the middle of the day it was cold.

Polish guards stood at every corner of our ghetto. They were called "Volksdeutsch." Their ancestors had originally come from Germany, and they were particularly proud of that. They lorded it over other Poles; those of Slavic ancestry. As for us Jews, there was nothing but contempt.

For the first few days, life in the ghetto was fairly idle. We were only allowed to walk around during daylight hours— not that there was much to see or do in so small a space.

Before too long, our main preoccupation was with food. We weren't allowed to leave the ghetto. Even when some food was distributed, it was far too little and in some cases, inedible. I tried to ignore the persistent knot of hunger in my stomach, but sometimes food was all I could think about. Often, when there was too little food, my mother gave us her portion to share, and went without. Every time I looked at Momma I shuddered. She was wasting away, not only from hunger, but also from a hopelessness that gripped her. She seemed lost somehow, and I wondered if she thought about my Poppa and wished that he were there so she could look to him to take care of us. Sometimes the despondent look on her face changed and she grabbed one of us and held us tightly to her breast; I could feel both love and despair in her embrace.

I began stealing food for my family. Being younger and smaller, it was easier for me to sneak out of the ghetto. I crept through the streets to the back alley behind the bakery where the fresh loaves of bread were cooling on the open windowsill. I always tried to take two loaves—one for us and one for Bubbe and Zayde, who'd been crammed into a small room not far from us. When I returned to the ghetto, I would put the bread in Momma's hands. Thank God she never asked me where it came from. How could I have explained that I was breaking the eighth commandment? As desperate as we were, I still wished to please God.

CHAPTER SEVEN

CHOOSING LIFE

One day, as Sarah and I walked through the ghetto street to visit our grandparents, she suddenly grabbed my arm. "What's going on over there?" she asked. I look where she was pointing and saw a gathering of people around one of the Volksdeutsch, who was reading aloud some kind of proclamation.

We couldn't hear him very well, but this same notice was pasted on the walls of buildings throughout the ghetto. Sarah and I walked over to read one ourselves—it was a call for laborers. If we were willing to work, it said, we could provide safety for our families.

"What do you think? Sarah asked me.

"If we can save Bubbe and Momma and Zayde, I don't think we have a choice."

"I think so, too."

"Besides," I said, "What else are we going to do?" I looked around. There was no more public school, no more Hebrew school. We had no garden to cultivate, no animals to tend. We couldn't just keep sitting around waiting for the next empty hour to come and go.

So we signed up. We chose life, for our families and ourselves. They told us to assemble in the marketplace early the next morning. When we arrived, German soldiers marched us to a factory under heavy guard. I don't know how far it was, but it seemed like we walked for hours. At last we arrived at an ammunition factory.

What did two girls aged eleven and thirteen know about live ammunition, factory work or machinery? A foreman, hastily showed us how to operate the machines. It was a simple lesson, and we had no choice but to learn correctly the first time. The guards watched over us menacingly, with weapons in hand. I paid close attention, as though my life depended on it—because it did. I didn't really understand the concept of death, but I knew I didn't want to be put into the ground like Poppa. I knew the guards would have no problem sending me there.

Sarah and I had different jobs. I worked on a stretching machine that lengthened shell casings to the size of rifle bullets. Sarah worked on a machine called a *Lackmaschine*, which sprayed a hot lacquer or varnish over the shell casings. It had to be very hot, and the casings sometimes fell on her lap, burning her badly. It hurt her so much, I couldn't understand how she still walked. She was such a delicate girl.

Momma always reminded Sarah to look after me, Luba, her little sister. "No matter what happens," she used to say, "as the older sister, you're responsible." In the factory, the roles began to reverse. I took on the responsibility of protecting Sarah as much as I could. I was the tough one. If she fell behind in her work, I would say something to distract the guards and get smacked for speaking. I really didn't care if they hurt me as long as Sarah was spared.

The beatings started almost immediately. We were slapped and punched and kicked. They pulled our hair. Some guards carried sticks, others used whips, which were cat-o-nine tails usually. These whips were made of nine knotted cords fastened to a handle. They applied the whips indiscriminately to anyone within arm's reach. Whether we were sitting, standing or climbing a ladder, the whip reached us. It struck our stomachs, our shoulders and our legs. It especially hurt when the whip struck your legs. It felt like an electric shock went right through you. But you had to continue working as if nothing had happened. The beatings became a routine part of the day; a way to keep us under control.

One day after work, they didn't march us back to the ghetto. They took us in a different direction for a long time, until we came to a camp set up with barracks. They opened the doors and ordered us to move inside. Each barrack contained rows of cots. We fell onto them, exhausted.

We never returned to the ghetto. The Proclamation had been a lie.

PART THREE

WAKING NIGHTMARES

CHAPTER EIGHT

FURTHER INTO DARKNESS

Sarah and I found ourselves in a hell made by man called Camp B. That first night, I cried for Momma, whom I missed terribly. When we cried or complained, we were whipped. But try reasoning with a little girl when she can't find her mother.

We continued to work about eighteen hours a day. We had to stay at the machines all that time. I was often so tired that the temptation to lay my head down briefly on my arms was too great, but if I was caught doing so, I'd be brutally woken.

Everything seemed to grow grayer. Our clothes became torn and stained with blood and grime. One day, I looked down at the pleated yellow skirt I wore. It used to be such a bright yellow—but now it was dingy and rumpled and sad. The blouse I wore had once been white, but you couldn't tell. It was so dirty. I was dirty.

Other Jews started arriving daily from Krakow and other parts of Poland. Some wore beautiful coats, elegant leather shoes, and long dresses of fine, floral-printed materials. But each lovely coat I saw had a line of white paint streaked down the back. What a waste, I thought naively, to ruin a good coat like that.

But these new arrivals didn't stay for long. The people disappeared, and some of their clothes reappeared, dumped unceremoniously in a pile on the cold floor. Oh, how we grabbed anything we could, especially a coat or a pair of shoes! As I hunted desperately for anything that would keep me and Sarah warm, I tried not to think of the people who had worn them and what might have happened to them.

Sometimes we heard a scream from someone who suddenly recognized the clothing of a family member. As each truckload of clothes came in, we slowly began to realize what this meant: a town or neighborhood had been emptied of Jews.

We later found out that all of these people were sent to the death camp Treblinka. That's where my family went—to Treblinka to be killed. My aunts, my uncles, my big brother, Nathan and my little sister, Esther, my Momma, my Bubbe, my Zayde, most of my cousins. All murdered. In less than a sentence they are gone.

My brother was the oldest. The apple of my parents' eye, he was my boss after my father died. I wanted to fight him all the time. But he was protective of me and all of us. He would come running to let me know when Momma was looking for me. "You're in trouble. Why are you climbing the roof? Why are you doing such things?"

Esther was the sweetest, the most beautiful human being that you could ever meet in your life. She never saw bad in others. Everyone was her friend and everyone was wonderful. She was blonde, dimples, blue eyes. Milk and butter her skin, rose cheeks. She was 3 or 4 years younger than me. I felt so guilty throughout the war that I could not bring her through with me.

And yet we still grabbed for the clothes.

The long, tormented night now really began. And of those years, isolated horrors stand out. Once, as I stood at my machine working, doing everything as it should be done, the foreman picked up his whip and began to hit me. It hurt so badly I almost passed out. I must have been crazy with pain and fear; I looked up at him and cried, "Why? Why are you hitting me? What did I do?"

He grabbed me by the arm and dragged me to the middle of the factory floor. Other guards surrounded me. They were from the Ukraine and worse than the Germans in their cruelty.

For the rest of the day, I was publicly beaten. Every time I dropped to the floor, they would pick me up and hold me upright and whip me again. Through the haze of pain and torment, I remember seeing Sarah across the factory floor. She was sobbing even as she worked. I so badly wanted to call out to her, but didn't want to draw attention to her for fear that she would be punished for her tears.

It is a special kind of sadism that punishes people just for being weak or upset or merely for asking why. I learned my lesson that day. I never asked any questions again in the camps. I still have a phobia about asking people questions. I even have a hard time asking people where they come from or what they do.

Of course that day I missed my quota of work. There were no acceptable reasons for missing one's quota. So that night I was put back at my machine. I worked through the dark until dawn to make up the previous day's quota of bullet casings. The next morning, with only two hours of sleep, I was at work again, as if nothing had happened.

Our daily food ration consisted of one slice of bread a quarter inch thick, a cup of chicory coffee and sometimes a cup of lentil soup. We knew it was soup because it was hot. We knew it was lentil soup because sometimes we saw a lentil float by.

We were all aware of the executions that occurred daily. One morning we were lined up outside the barracks. Along with some others, I was called out of line and told to stand in another line. It was the bad line; we all knew that. It was my turn to be killed. I saw my Sarah's face grow pale. She motioned to me to come back to her. But we were being heavily guarded, and I couldn't risk them killing us both.

Suddenly there was a brief moment when the guards were preoccupied with something, and I felt somebody pull me out of the line. I didn't look to see who it was, I just ran blindly towards the barracks and managed to squeeze my body underneath the structure. I huddled there, trying not to breathe or cry or do anything that would give away my hiding place. I felt like a hunted animal.

In that moment I made a decision. I would not let myself die. Looking back, that seems absurd. After all, I was in so many ways helpless against the forces that wanted to snuff out my life. But somehow that inner resolution gave me strength. "I will not die," I repeated to myself.

I stayed under the barracks all night, not daring to fall asleep. As I made myself as close to the ground as possible, I realized that these barracks were built on the same wooded ground where I had once played with my brother and sisters and friends only months earlier. I remembered how when we played in these woods, certain places had been designated "safe." Nobody could touch you if you were in a "safe" place. Now, as I lay in the dirt, frightened and cold, it occurred to me that I hadn't felt safe in a very long time.

Early the next morning I crept back inside and made my way stealthily to Sarah, who cried when she saw me.

"Rose!"

"Shhhhhh, someone might hear!"

"You poor thing, you are ice cold."

"I know and we have to leave for the factory soon," I moaned.

I knew I had to go to work. I couldn't stay at the barracks and let someone find me; it was too risky. But my body ached so badly from malnutrition and beatings and exhaustion and fear that I couldn't move. Before I knew it, I was asleep. And I slept there on my cot the whole day, curled up in the fetal position. It was a miracle to me.

The next day when I went back to the factory, someone was at my machine. She stepped away when she saw me, and I took up my old place. It felt weird to have missed a day of work. I almost expected a benevolent teacher to inquire about my health, and catch me up on my homework, like in the old days. But of course, nobody did.

A few days after my close call with the selection line, the Commandant of the camp came into the factory. He walked over to my machine and stared at me as I worked. I tried with all my might not to tremble under his gaze.

He walked around and stood behind me. "Stand up," he ordered. I did so and wondered silently if this was going to be the end of me. The Commandant called over a couple of guards and began whispering to them while I stood there motionless. They all nodded in agreement.

The next thing I knew, I was being taken to the "watch tower." It was a guardhouse, not really a tower. I was told that my new job was to feed the geese and the livestock penned behind it. I had no idea why my assignment was changed. I was scared to be taken away from Sarah. But my new job had its benefits, I discovered.

Regularly, as I went to the watchtower, I passed the place where they steamed potatoes that sometimes went into our measly rations of food. My yellow skirt came in handy then. I would take one potato for the geese and two potatoes for me. One for them, two for me. After filling my skirt with potatoes, I would run back to the barracks and hide them before the others returned from the factory. Then I ran back to the guardhouse, fed the geese, ran to get more potatoes, and rushed back to the barracks. When the other prisoners returned, I would sit there clothed in my secret knowledge as if I were disguised royalty. After all, I was rich; I had potatoes. Some of my cousins were still alive at that time, living in the barracks with me. We shared the food among us.

It's difficult now to understand how possession of a few potatoes can change one's perspective. I felt as if God had his hand on me. But then someone told the guards that I possessed this bounty. Was it a fellow prisoner, jealous and unwilling to grant my cousins and me the few extra

carbohydrates per day? Certainly she had nothing to gain.
Or maybe she was rewarded with a few potatoes herself.

Either way, I received a terrible beating that day.
Guards came and dragged me outside. The Commandant
was there, looking madder than I had ever seen him.
Later, I found out that the reason I had been given my new
job was because I looked like his daughter, and he
couldn't stand that someone who resembled her would
steal. Seeing someone who looked like his daughter
beaten within an inch of her life didn't seem to disturb
him. I'll never understand the contradiction.

CHAPTER NINE

A STOLEN CHILDHOOD

Obviously, I was never allowed near the guardhouse again. And the nightmare began to worsen with each passing day. Why they didn't shoot me after the potato incident, I'll never know. People were killed for far less.

We were also forced to watch many public hangings. One day, the young woman who was executed was particularly beautiful. They stripped her naked and hung her. We all had to watch until her body stopped jerking. She was chosen, we were told, as an example. "Do not behave the way she did," we were told. I'd never seen her behave differently from the rest of us, but I knew somehow that her beauty had caused her death. I myself didn't feel beautiful, but I began to think, "How can I behave so as not to look beautiful?" It was far better to be ugly, like everything else.

I am about to share something that haunts me to this day. On Saturday afternoons, they would march some of us to a building, up to the second floor. This was called the "upper room." This was the soldiers' entertainment room, much like a cafe or a beer hall in Vienna. Our hands were tied, and we were hung from the rafters, like sides of beef. We were swung around and flogged with a cat-o-nine tails. Where it struck, the skin would tear open, like scratches from a cat.

Soldiers sat around drinking beer, smoking cigarettes, laughing and joking. They made bets as to who would scream the loudest. If we didn't scream loud enough, they might cut us down and tie us on a "stretching table." They tied our hands over our heads at one end, and our feet around a piece of wood with a handle on it at the other. Then they would crank the handle, stretching our limbs apart until we could scream no more.

Many women died on that table. Many died from other tortures. Blood splattered the walls and the floor of that room. To this day I see it and smell it.

I don't know that I ever suffered more than when my sister was taken to the upper room. Herring, a large German master with greasy, dark hair and stained teeth that twisted into a grotesque smile, particularly delighted in mistreating Sarah. He was unbelievably cruel to her, and when she cried and pleaded for mercy, he took her to the upper room. As I watched her being dragged off, a scream rose inside of me: "Take me! Don't take her! She's too frail!" But it didn't matter.

There is no way to describe how it feels to know that men are deriving pleasure from inflicting intense pain. Their faces lighted up, their eyes glinted, their foreheads and cheeks shone from dried sweat.

Only now have I come to know this behavior has a name—sadism. These men derived a perverse satisfaction from inflicting pain on others. Faces like these surrounded us for my entire adolescence. I came to think that they were the norm.

I came to think of abject cruelty and fear as normal. You never knew when a random bullet might end your life. You never knew who might grab you and do things that no human being should do to another. Rape was common. This was how we lived.

Children were abused and beaten more than the others. Why? I didn't know then, and I don't know now how people can do such things to children. I don't know how you can look at something as innocent and beautiful as a child and decide to tear it to pieces. I just don't know.

The guards frequently lined all of us five deep and counted us. They counted us over and over and it seemed to take forever. During each roll call, they would select people out of the lines. We never saw those people again. They moved from the deathlike existence we all shared to their graves. There was no rationale behind it, no rhyme or reason that could possibly explain why certain people were killed at certain times. We were all guilty of only one crime—being Jewish. Our mere presence was an offense worthy of death.

Even though I could never vocalize my questions, inwardly my mind raged at times. Why didn't anyone like me anymore? What had I done? Had the pranks I'd played as a youngster generated such hate? Why was I a prisoner near the very town where I'd been born and raised?

There were no answers to my questions. Since there were no answers, I would have settled for comfort. So I prayed, "God of Abraham, Isaac, and Jacob, help me. I need a hug. I need a hug from my Momma, my Bubbe and my Zayde."

But they were gone, and I knew they would never hold me again. It was useless to pray, I thought. It was useless to believe in such a silent God.

I decided that my mother was misguided, or at worst, she had lied to me. And my revered Zayde? He hadn't taught me the right things. If there was a loving God, I would not be here, being treated worse than an animal.

And I realized suddenly, there was no God. If I were to survive, it would have to be on my own. If anyone was going to protect Sarah, it would have to be me.

There was no God, but there was a hell. It was not a lake of fire, but as Dante describes it, a frozen lake at the center of which sits Satan. We lived through such a hell those miserable winters in the camp. And through the damp bite of spring and the chilling gusts of fall, our scant clothes provided little warmth to our malnourished bodies. Even during blistering summer days, our spirits found no warmth.

And I was no longer a child.

My adolescence vanished in a miasma of pain and hunger. When I should have been at dances or out on dates, I was gnawing at raw potatoes, trying to survive. I was not a teenager, and there were days when I barely believed I was a person.

CHAPTER TEN

HUNGER

Sarah and I were transferred to Camp A. The Nazis had set up three camps in our small town, camps A, B and C. The conditions and the work were the same. The only discernible difference was that the machines didn't break down as often in Camp A.

Each barracks building contained rows of narrow bunks made of wood, stacked in tiers of three. Sarah and I chose a top bunk together. At night, my head was always pressed up near someone else's head or feet. Bathroom facilities were crude and sparse. During the night urine would sometimes stream down from the upper bunks.

As we arrived, my weary eyes took in the surroundings. Suddenly my eyes fell on a familiar face. "Auntie Dora!" I called out to her and waved. Sarah and I went over to her, and I felt my heart lift a bit at the sight of a family member. Dora was my mother's sister.

It was a glimmer of hope. Surely things would be better, easier somehow. I believed that any member of my family would help us, shelter us. Some I knew, would have given their lives for us.

Aunt Dora looked pleased to see us, but she was far from effusive. That night, as Sarah and I lay in the bunk, I whispered to her, "Did you see how much food Auntie Dora had stashed?"

"I know!" Sarah whispered back. "Do you think she'll share it with us?"

But Aunt Dora never offered either Sarah or me any of her food. At first I couldn't understand how she could ignore us, children from her own sister's womb. But this wasn't real life; this was survival. And each of us did what we had to do. All of the social norms, the usual politeness, the concern for others vanished quickly at the sight or smell of food.

We lived for food, and we died for food. It was an obsession. Our hunger never left us. Even after we ate our ration of food, we ached for more. I dreamed of food.

Documents show that the average prisoner's diet in the camps consisted of less than eight hundred calories per day. Life cannot be sustained on so little. An interesting fact surfaced after the war about the gruel served prisoners in some camps. I found that one of the main ingredients of the bread they gave us was sawdust. I don't know what kind of mind thinks of such a thing.

Our hunger was so insistent that we rarely kept food. But one night, I hid a piece of bread under my thin pillow so Sarah and I could share it in the morning.

During the night a sound woke me, and I felt something moving near my arm. I lifted the pillow and saw a rat gnawing on the piece of bread. "No!" I gestured wildly, chasing the rat away, and waking up a woman near me. She looked at me as I held the half chewed piece of bread in my hand, sick at the thought of eating what a rat had eaten first, but still so hungry.

"Don't throw it away," the woman hissed.

"But the rat . . ." I protested miserably.

"It's food," she said firmly. "Besides, if you eat the parts the rat was chewing on, you'll have strong teeth."

Her advice, whether she meant it or not, suddenly reminded me of something my Bubbe would say. And even though my body shuddered at what diseases that rat might have been carrying, I knew the woman was right: It was food. It would get Sarah and me through another day.

From Camp A it took us longer to walk to the factory for work. Sometimes as we marched, I would steal a glance of the sky above. It was getting harder and harder to comprehend that there was a world beyond the camp. The outside world and my memories of it seemed to disappear. It was too painful to remember that there had once been a time when my body was clean, my stomach was full and my family was around me.

One day as I walked, something another young woman said or did actually made me smile. It was a strange sensation, to feel my cheeks pull up and my teeth exposed. It didn't last long, however.

"You! Jew-girl, what are you smiling about!" a guard shouted as he towered over me.

I didn't have a chance to say anything before he grabbed me and beat me severely. I actually felt my skin tear off. I can still feel it.

Afterwards he looked at me and sneered, "I'll give you something to smile about, Jew-girl."

Then he and another guard dragged me off and threw me into a tank full of raw sewage. The smell was horrendous. I cannot even think about it without getting sick. But far worse was the toll it took on my body. I developed large sores that wouldn't heal.

A cut on my thumb became infected and a red mark appeared on my arm, almost like a welt. One night the same woman who had persuaded me to eat the rat-bread looked at it and grimaced. "Gangrene," she said. She told me to urinate on my thumb, and it might get better. I did just as she told me, and my thumb healed. I will never forget this woman; she probably saved my arm.

One night as we stood in line for soup, Sarah whispered excitedly that she'd heard our Uncle Meyer was somewhere in Camp A. My heart soared at the thought of that debonair and gentle young man.

Uncle Meyer's wife was also in the camp. One day she prevailed on him to try to get her more bread. He was shot and killed during the attempt. When I found out, I wanted to tear Lubah's heart out. I had blamed her for taking Uncle Meyer away from me in the first place, and now she had taken him away forever.

But the mere prospect of food can make a starving person do extreme things. I remember the day I was called into the camp Commandant's office. Before that, I had only seen him from a distance. Up close, he was an ugly man, short with a hunched back. I was almost as tall as him. Rumors of his cruelty were well known. I tried not to show my fear as I entered his office.

He looked at me silently for a couple of minutes. Then he got up from his desk, and walked slowly toward me, his gaze fixed on my face.

"Tell me," he said, "Who are the people in the Underground in our camp? We must have their names!" He spoke imperiously yet seductively as he said *our* camp. As if we were in a proprietary arrangement, he and I.

I mumbled that I didn't know. The Underground was a secret group of people working for the resistance. I had heard vaguely of them, but I had no idea who they were. The whole idea was a mystery to me. Their existence was cause for both hope and anxiety.

"Well, you will find out for me then," he replied. "That is, if you want to live." He told me to open my hands and in them he slowly placed four eggs, one at a time. The message was clear. If I spied for him, he would give me food. If not—well, there was no "if not." I had the vague sense that he expected four people's names in exchange, one for each egg.

Without another word, he dismissed me. During the next few days, I spent as much time as possible hiding inside the toilet. I thought that if members of the Underground found me, they might kill me. I thought that the Commandant might order me killed for not being aggressive enough in my "spying."

But the eggs were good; the best I ever remembered tasting. I shared them with Sarah and my cousins.

It took very little to get people to betray each other in the concentration camp. Usually the promise of food was enough for someone to turn on another. And those who turned in exchange for privileges were often the cruelest. There was a German Jew whom we called "Viteda" who functioned as watchman over us. He was working for the Nazis in order to survive. Viteda wasn't his real name, but we called him that because he was constantly shouting at us to "Viteda!—Keep going!" He beat us constantly. His whip had steel fringes on the bottom, which I think he'd added himself. It was hard to believe that a Jewish man could treat us the way he did, just so he could curry favor with the Nazis. He even knew our family somehow, but he beat Sarah and me with the same ferocity as he beat the others. I later learned he was killed by other prisoners in Buchenwald. In the end, his brutal, traitorous efforts had counted for nothing.

As for me, I never gave the Commandant any information. I remember him standing at the gate as people left the factory. At times, he would personally inspect everyone, perhaps for stolen ammunition, who knows? Then suddenly, a month or so after my appointment in his office, he disappeared from camp altogether. To this day, I don't know why.

But soon after that, a group of young men were caught trying to escape the camp. We were all called out of the barracks, and lined up in orderly rows so everyone could see the gallows in the middle of the camp. It was before dinner so our stomachs were insistent. Irrationally, perhaps insanely, I resented these men for delaying our meal and wished that the hangings would be over soon so we could eat. Such were the depths we were reduced to.

The gallows was a crude affair, a raised wooden platform on which a horizontal beam was supported by vertical

beams at each end. Ropes hung down from the beam. The
prisoners were obliged to step up onto wooden stools.
When nooses had been slipped over the young men's heads,
some official spoke to us, the spectators, the assembled
prisoners. He preached a cautionary tale—the danger of
disobedience. The lesson I learned? Your only choice was to
die trying to live, or to live a slow death.

A guard then kicked the stools out from under each
young man. As he worked his way down the row, the legs of
the preceding boys flailed briefly, vainly searching for
support as their breath was cut off. Their movements
decreased, their eyes rolled back in their eye sockets, and
their tongues lolled out of their mouths, turning blue.
Watching them was agony.

An extra portion of bread was served with the soup
that night.

CHAPTER ELEVEN

TRANSPORT

"Everybody out! Now! Move!" The shouting woke us and the barracks instantly became full of activity, like a hornet's nest. We all stumbled over each other as the guards pushed and hit us, driving us out of the barracks before we were even fully awake. They marched us swiftly to the train tracks, where we saw a series of cattle cars with open doors. I raised my head to see that they were empty. Each car had a bucket in the corner.

They stuffed as many people as they could into cattle cars and then continued to cram even more bodies inside. We were crushed together so tightly I could barely breathe. Then we began to pull away. It was so packed in the car that we all had to stand practically on top of each other. There was no room to maneuver to the bucket that was meant for us to urinate and defecate in, so we just urinated standing where we were and felt it dry on our legs. The air quickly became foul and some people passed out.

"Rose, where are we going?" Sarah asked, her voice muffled as she tried to use her hand to guard her nose from the acrid smell.

"I don't know. I don't know if I want to know." And it was true. I detested Camp A and wanted wholeheartedly to believe that we would be taken some place better. At the same time, fear of the unknown made me reluctant to leave Camp A.

There was so little light in the cattle car that it was hard to tell, but it seemed as though we traveled all day towards

our unknown destination, which turned out to be
Chenstochov, another concentration camp.

When we arrived at the new camp, and stumbled out of
the car, we were immediately divided into different groups.
I was put in a group of young people, some my age, some
slightly older, but I was still with Sarah, which was all that
mattered to me.

They marched us to a two-story building, and up to the
second floor, another factory. We were put to work making
ammunition again. The Nazis were coming under pressure
from the Allies; they were speeding up ammunitions
production, so we had to work even longer hours. The beatings
lessened a bit, as there was a need to keep all of us working.

At Chenstochov, the machines we operated were never
maintained. Sometimes they broke down or exploded.
Many younger ones working those machines were maimed
or killed in this way. If you were maimed and couldn't
work, you were shot.

It was often bitter cold, even indoors. I could barely
feel my fingers as I worked. The food was about the same.
There was never enough, so every day our bodies
consumed themselves a little more. As we wasted away, we
worked less perfectly. We all knew that we couldn't keep
working like this for much longer; eventually we would
give out and be replaced.

One particularly tiring day, I was working as usual, trying
to meet my quota, when suddenly the machine I was using
exploded. Sparks flew and pieces of shrapnel pierced my
leg and back. Before I could scream with pain, somebody
grabbed me, clapped a hand over my mouth, carried me to
the other room, and lifted me onto a table. Somebody else
pushed a rag, into my mouth so I couldn't make noise and
attract the attention of the guards.

"Shhhh! If they find out you're hurt, they won't need you
anymore! And then ..." the stranger left his sentence
unfinished. But I understood.

A prisoner began "working" on my leg with a knife to remove pieces of metal. I kept hearing him murmur, "Another one, another one." As he worked as fast as he could, someone else held my hands and slapped my face to distract me from the pain in my leg. It worked. They bandaged me with rags and put me back near the machine while they tried to repair it. After all, the quota must be met. I stood there dazed, bleeding. But then I must have gone into shock because I don't remember what happened next.

When I came to my senses, I was in the barracks. I dragged myself outside and found myself a corner, a small niche, under the wooden structure. Though it was dark and damp, I felt sheltered, if only for a brief time. Through the pain, hunger, exhaustion and filth I thought to myself, "Look at me, I am the dirty Jew they said I was." It had been ages since I'd seen myself in a mirror but I knew I wouldn't be deemed fit to sit at a table with civilized company. Hiding under the barracks, I felt like the vermin they said we were.

"God," I whispered, "Please, tell me you're there. Tell me you love me." I waited, but heard and felt nothing.

"God!" I cried, "I want to go back to my Momma. I don't want to be here anymore. Please God of Abraham, Isaac and Jacob, let me go back to my Momma!"

But again, God was silent.

I returned to my bunk in the barracks, trying not to wake Sarah. I knew I had to show up at the machine again and keep working. After a couple of days, the bleeding stopped, but pus began oozing from the cuts. The pain was unbearable, but I wasn't allowed to sit or lie down. A simple equation ruled our lives: work or die. I was burning up with fever, and so weak that sometimes I fell to the floor. Someone always picked me up, held me, and gave me a drink of water. At one point, I had to go to the toilet. I knew I could rest there a minute. As I went in, I collapsed in the booth and fell asleep from exhaustion.

Suddenly I felt someone shaking me violently. Sarah was screaming, "Get up, get up!" She took me by the hand, and lifting me up, led me back to the machine. As I leaned against it for support, words went through my mind. "I must survive this hell. No matter what they do to me, I will survive!"

From that time on, I became strong. I didn't feel the pain as much. I didn't feel the fever. I knew I had to survive, and the only way was to work and to harden myself.

One night, Sarah said to me, "Do you know what tomorrow is?" I shrugged. "It's Rosh Hashanah." I shrugged again. What did the new year mean to me except that I was still in this wretched place? All it meant was that more time had passed; more of my life had been eaten away. Marking time only mattered when there was an end in sight. What was the point of Rosh Hashanah when it seemed there would be no sweetness in the new year?

Ten days after Rosh Hashanah came Yom Kippur. Ironically, we were served an extra meal on our holy fast day. As I reached to take my portion of food, Sarah grabbed my arm. "Rose! It's Yom Kippur!"

"I know that, Sarah. Don't tell me you're actually going to fast!"

"Of course," she insisted.

"Are you crazy?" I shouted at her. "You need to eat!"

"But it's Yom Kippur," she repeated. I wanted so badly to strangle her. She was so thin, so weak, and this food would help her, at least for another day. But I looked into her eyes and knew I wasn't going to change her mind.

"Fine, you fast," I scoffed. "But there's no way I'm going to."

Sarah wasn't the only one who refused to eat. Others beckoned me to fast too. I shrugged them off.

"There is no God who will make me fast," I said bluntly. Some of the women looked at me sadly, but I didn't care. How was I supposed to believe in God, let alone obey him, when he was allowing such misery? How was I supposed to believe that he cared about me or any of us?

I made Sarah take a portion of food, and I watched over it for her until Yom Kippur ended.

I could feel a coldness spreading through my heart, as though it had frostbite. But I didn't care. Let people think I was hard and uncaring. It was better than them pitying me and saying, "That poor little child."

Chenstochov was my school of survival. It was also where I finally gave up my faith.

Word reached us that our entire city was "Judenrein." That meant that every Jew had been cleared from the city. The Germans and the Poles took pride in declaring an area "Judenrein." All the Jews of my city had been taken to Treblinka and killed. We were now a remnant, left to die more slowly.

As I fully realized I would never again see my family I cried hard and long until all the tears left me. Then came tearless sobs of despair, almost silent screams. My mouth formed the word "why" over and over, but no sound escaped my throat. And then I was done. From then on, I kept my emotions inside and my heart grew steadily colder.

One morning soon after, the camp hummed with secret excitement—the Russians were coming! The rumors raced around the camp like field mice and we began to hope that the Russian army was advancing as quickly. It was 1944 by that time. I had spent four years in concentration camps.

Each of us was given a whole loaf of bread, an unheard of feast, and then we were herded onto trains again. This time we all somehow knew our destination—Germany.

We later found out that just as we left, the Russians entered the other side of town. We just barely missed being liberated.

We were shunted from train to train, from camp to camp. On the trains we had to fight to survive. I had taken the loaves of bread given to Sarah and me, and hidden them under my clothes near my belly. During the night, as I tried to catch a precious hour's sleep, I felt a hand reaching across my belly, grabbing for the bread. I grabbed that hand and bit it as hard as I could. A woman screamed and cursed in pain. She was one of two sisters who also survived. I believe they now live in Rochester, New York. To this day, she must carry my teeth marks on her hand. We had become animals.

We were on the trains for three or four weeks. The conditions were horrible. The bread we hoarded was finally gone. The smell was unbearable; the car was filthy with sewage. There was no privacy.

And we were so thirsty. Occasionally we were given muddy water to drink out of a bucket, but it was never enough and it stank and there were always unrecognizable things floating in it. When it rained or snowed, we would stick our hand out between the slits in the sides of the train car just to capture a few drops in our palms, and lick the precious dampness.

When the track was clear, the trains moved. But sometimes the cars of human cargo just sat for hours on a railroad siding, either because the tracks had been destroyed or because we were under orders to wait. When the train was stopped, they would sometimes let us off to stretch our legs, or to go behind a bush to urinate or move our bowels. We were in such a weakened state, I guess the guards figured we'd never manage to run away.

We were deep in Germany when the train finally arrived at our destination. As soon as the train car doors swung open, guards herded us onto the platform and began separating out the men. I glanced up and saw a sign—we had arrived at Buchenwald.

As they sifted through our exhausted group and pulled the men aside, we knew they were as good as dead. Their journey was over. As for the rest of us, the guards pushed us back onto the train. Again there was no water or food. We were so weak that many of us eliminated where we stood or lay. What was the use of getting up? The whole train was a sewer.

Once again, the train stopped and the doors opened. The cold air rushed in and we piled out of the car, practically dead on our feet. I looked up and saw another sign. We were now in Bergen-Belsen.

CHAPTER TWELVE

BERGEN-BELSEN

Of all the places I was imprisoned, Bergen-Belsen was the worst, though we stayed there the shortest amount of time. Things were done to me there that even my sister doesn't know about. And I will never tell her. I will not share them with you either.

I will tell you that it was winter when we arrived, the winter of 1944-1945. It was bitter cold. As soon as we left the train, guards ordered us to take off all our clothes and dump them in front of us. Then they tossed each of us a blue and gray uniform. I tried not to think about the fact that somebody else had once worn this uniform and what had most certainly happened to her. Maybe many others had worn it, before—no, I could not think of it. This was my clothing now and I quickly covered my naked body with it. Someone threw me a coat, or rather, a large robe. It was so long, it dragged on the ground. Sarah tore off the bottom for me to use as a belt. Her robe was also long and way too big for her small frame. We could both wrap the robes around us twice and keep them in place with the belts Sarah made.

This double layer kept us slightly warmer. Our first job at Bergen-Belsen was not inside a factory, but outside, digging up sugar beets. The earth was frozen; we had to dig out the sugar beets with our hands. We clawed and spaded the frozen earth with our fingers, which soon were bruised and raw and frozen. I managed to hide some of the beets in the double layer of my robe. My vivid imagination changed the beets into whatever I wanted them to be. One bite of the raw beet was a piece of cheese; the next was a chicken wing. Those beets tasted that good. When I was caught, I was beaten terribly, but it was worth it.

We were fed just enough to keep us alive so that we could work. The ration of bread per day was one slice about the size of a piece of American white bread. Later, I was told that some days the bread was 65 to 85 percent sawdust. We washed our piece of bread down with a cup of chicory coffee.

At the end of every day, they assembled all of the prisoners in rows, selected several people and marched them off. We never saw them again; it was like they just disappeared. The crematoria burned constantly, day and night, forever reminding us that we might be the ones selected next time.

Those of us left alive had other horrors foisted upon us. I hesitate to write this next part, because I know that when Sarah reads this account, it will be the first time she hears what was done to me. One icy morning, we were lined up in fives for roll call as usual. When a guard motioned to me, I was taken out of line. I thought surely this was it—I would be marched to the crematorium. But instead I and the other girls who were selected were taken to a snowy field where the guards stripped us naked. Then they buried us in snow up to our waists. It was an "experiment" to see how long it takes for blood to freeze. Every once in awhile someone would come and draw our blood to measure its temperature. In the meantime, we stood clustered together in the snow, our upper bodies resembling candles in the white frosting of a birthday cake. It wasn't long before some of the "candles" were snuffed out. Those who fell around me, or whose bodies leaned on me like wilted weeds, gave me their dim flame of warmth. They sustained my life even after they gave up theirs. After what seemed like many hours, the attendants grew weary or decided that the experiment had yielded sufficient results. Other prisoners came to take those still living inside and to dispose of the dead. I do not remember much of what happened after we were taken inside that day. I remember that my body was numb and an eerie bluish color and as the numbness wore off there was intense pain. Other than that all I can remember is that I scarcely believed I was still alive.

CHAPTER THIRTEEN

SAVING SARAH

In early1945, the allies were destroying the Nazi war machine faster than it could be rebuilt. There were no more ammunition factories to work in and no more beets to pull up, so Sarah and I felt useless. We weren't needed or wanted at Bergen-Belsen anymore, so once again we were put on a train that took us deeper into Germany and stopped at a place called Berguille, part of the Dachau concentration camp.

As Sarah and I were trying to settle into a top bunk, I noticed that she seemed weaker than usual and her face looked flush. Then I saw a rash on her arms and hands. "Sarah, lie down," I told her. "You don't look well at all."

It turned out that Sarah had contracted typhoid fever. Thousands had died from an epidemic of the dread disease, yet it was vitally important for Sarah to look as healthy as possible. But her condition worsened to the point where she couldn't even keep food down. I fed her tiny pieces of bread, patiently putting them in her mouth, willing her to swallow while I stroked her chestnut hair.

The guards were on fierce lookout for anyone who had the fever, so when they came to inspect the barracks, I put my threadbare blanket over Sarah and laid on top of her. The guards had each of us show our hands from the bunks so they could inspect them for rashes. I held out my hands and remained on top of my sister until they finally left.

She was safe for the time being, but her fever continued to worsen. Her skin felt like a flame to the touch. "She needs medicine, probably aspirin," said a woman in our barracks. "Where am I supposed to get medicine?" I protested. The woman shrugged helplessly.

I could not let my Sarah die. That night, I waited until everyone was asleep and made my way in the dark to the infirmary. The fear that my sister would leave me overcame my fear of being caught. Still, my heart pounded in my ears. When I finally reached the infirmary, I discovered to my amazement that it wasn't locked. I took a deep breath and tiptoed inside. I expected at least the cabinets to be locked, but to my surprise, they too, were open. I don't know if someone just forgot to secure them, or if the Germans were simply confident that they'd broken our spirits to the point that we would never try to steal medicine. I grabbed as many bottles of pills as I could carry. I couldn't read the labels in German, so I raced back to the barracks and woke the woman who said Sarah needed aspirin. "Will this work?" I asked breathlessly. She took one of the bottles, read the label and nodded.

We pried open Sarah's mouth and forced her to swallow some tablets every few hours. Over the next few days her fever dropped, and she began to eat on her own again. Whatever she had left over I ate. And I never got sick! It was the first time in months that I thanked God for anything. But without my sister, I knew I wouldn't survive, so I silently, I thanked God for sparing her, both for her sake and for mine.

CHAPTER FOURTEEN

HOPING AGAINST HOPE

The German system was breaking down as the Allies continued to pummel them. And their confidence was ceasing as well. We could tell they didn't quite know what to do with all of us prisoners. We were sent to another camp, Türkheim, also part of Dachau. Stretched across the entrance, a large banner greeted us as we marched in: "YOU KILLED OUR GOD, JESUS CHRIST, AND NOW, WE KILL YOU."

But we didn't stay in Türkheim long; the Allies were advancing so rapidly and overrunning the German army and the fatherland with such speed that the Nazis were afraid to be caught with fresh evidence of genocide. We were put on another train, and sent to another part of Dachau. At first they wouldn't let us in. To some in the German administration, it must have seemed like a merchandising problem: "We have too much product; how can we quickly and efficiently dispose of it?"

Again we were put back on a cattle train, but we didn't get further than Schwabhausen, near Munich. From inside the train car, we could hear the roar of American bombers as they flew overhead and bombed the train. First, they bombed both ends of the tracks so the train couldn't move. The train itself was made up of many cars. Some carried ammunition that no doubt many of us trapped in the other

cars had slaved over. I couldn't get over the accuracy of the
American bombers—they hit only the cars filled with
ammunition. The noise and explosions were so loud that
some of us lost all sense of reality.

Finally, with explosions right and left, someone was able
to open the doors of the train car. Like wild animals we all
charged out and started running as fast as we could into the
woods. We passed through the woods, and ran into a small
town. We saw a barn at the edge of the town and ran for it.
Hanging from the rafters of the barn were freshly killed
hogs. Forgetting everything else, even the biblical injunction
against eating swine, we attacked the meat, gnawing at the
carcasses until we had gorged ourselves and our stomachs
ached. I ate until I got sick, and to this day I'm still allergic
to ham and pork.

German soldiers later found us lying there exhausted,
dazed and sick. They didn't shoot us, but marched us to
three barracks in the center of the field. We were shoved
inside, and the doors were bolted. We didn't know if the
guards stood outside or not, but we were too sick and weak
to attempt escape.

I don't know how long we stayed there. Too exhausted
to cry, too afraid to try and leave, we groaned, leaning
against or lying on top of one another. Urine flowed from
us from time to time, spreading across our legs, and seeping
into the German earth.

A few days later, through the slats in the barracks, we saw
tanks in the distance. Then we heard shouting in different
languages. Then the barracks doors opened.

We knew from their uniforms that they were American,
but we could scarcely believe it. They stared at us, aghast at
what they saw. These large, well-fed, battle-clad soldiers
could only gape silently, unable to comprehend what they
were seeing. Some had tears streaming down their faces.
We couldn't understand their English words, but some of
them showed us their stars of David or their *mezuzos*,

indicating that they too, were Jewish. They handed out candy bars, and cradled the smaller ones among us.

When a soldier first offered us a chocolate bar, I clapped my hand over my mouth and shook my head at Sarah. I thought it was a trick, perhaps poison. But then the soldiers started eating the candy themselves—and then there was no stopping us. I got sick, as did many others. Our stomachs weren't used to rich food.

For some of us, our first thoughts were not of freedom but of revenge. "It's time for us to get even!" someone said, and I felt a visceral, violent hatred surge through me. I wanted to murder the guards who had hit us and the townspeople who had complied. I even wanted to go into the town we were near and burn down the church—think how much we had suffered in the name of Jesus Christ. Irrationally, I thought that if I could burn down the church, I could put an end to Jesus, and an end to the hateful acts committed in his name.

But how equipped would we really be to enact revenge on anyone in our state? We were merely weary, hunger-crazed girls who could barely believe that we were being liberated. Was it true? Would there be no more barbed wire, barking dogs, whips or crematoria? Could we actually come and go as we wanted?

To be honest, it was hard for us to believe that we were worth liberating, Why would they come for us? Did our lives matter after all? Apparently so.

That thought gave me courage. I looked at Sarah and took her hand. "Sarah," I said, "It's time to go home."

My Momma-
Miriam Ronchka Feldman

Bubbe & Zayde-
Riva & Israel Ronchka

Uncle Meyer and Aunt Dora

My brother Nachum

The family, before the war. Left to right, starting in rear: Aunt Rose, Uncle Meyer, Aunt Helen, Uncle Herschel, Aunt Dora, Dora's husband, Aunt Sara, Sara's Husband, (bottom row) Great-Aunt (no name), Zayde, Bubbe, Aunt Helen's son Avram (sitting on Bubbe's lap), cousin Rachel and two other great-aunts

A get-together of the surviving cousins and their spouses

Left to right: Aunt Dora, Uncle Eleg and Aunt Rachel

My Husband Charlie and me at Candy's bat mitzvah in 1967

Left to right: My sister Sara, her son Harvey, daughter Mary and husband, Sam at Harvey's bar mitzvah

Rose speaking at "Berlin for Jesus," Olympic Stadium, Berlin, 1981.

Left: Our son, Norman,
with Charlie and me

Below left: Fred, Candie,
Sherah, Jonathan
and Chava

Below right: My daughter
Miriam with her two
daughters Jaffa and Natanya

My daughters Miriam and Candy

Me and my new husband, Jonathan

PART FOUR

COMING HOME

CHAPTER FIFTEEN

THE SEARCH BEGINS

I know that mine is one of millions of stories that could be told from the Holocaust, some of which we will never know because the men, women and children didn't survive to tell them. Among those were my mother, my Bubbe, my Zayde and many other relatives. I will never fully know what happened to them, what they thought, felt and experienced before they were systematically killed.

It's hard to reconstruct the precise sequence of events during the weeks and months that followed our liberation. I remember saying to Sarah, "Let's go home." The next thing I knew, I woke up in an unfamiliar room. I saw Sarah's face above me.

"Am I dead? Are we in heaven?"

Sarah smiled and spoke and it was the sweetest sound I'd ever heard: "No, Rose, baby sister, you aren't dead. You're in a convent, St. Tetelia; the Americans are using it for a hospital."

I said nothing further. I just took Sarah's hand and held it, grateful, so grateful, to be alive. Inside, I knew that part of my gratitude was due to the fact that I knew I wasn't ready to die. I wasn't ready to face the God that I had denied, if by some chance, he did exist after all. But I didn't dwell on it

too much then. I promptly fell right back to sleep, enjoying
the sheer bliss of rest.

When we were first herded into the ghetto in Poland, my
Zayde had made us promise that whatever happened, when
it was over, we would return to Skarzysko and meet at our
house. It was difficult to fathom that it might still exist, yet I
still remembered the street and the address. I'd said it over
and over to myself, so that I wouldn't forget.

At first, though, we were not free to go anywhere on our
own. The Americans gathered us up like wilted flowers, and
transported us to a Displaced Persons camp. Our DP camp
was called "Feldafing." There we found some of our cousins
and our Aunt Dora. What a joyous reunion. But years of
deprivation and fending for ourselves had taken their toll,
and it was clear we could no longer be as close as we had
once been. Cousin Esther took some of my cousins to
Stuttgart. Sarah and I were left to fend for ourselves.

My skin was finally healing, and the bruises that covered
my body were disappearing. I even gained a little weight.
The wilted flowers had been watered and nourished and
were beginning to open to the sun.

I began to feel restless at Feldafing, and eventually I
decided to leave. Sarah was doing much better health-wise
and seemed content enough to stay. I didn't know where I
was going. I was driven by the desire to try and find more
family members and by the intoxicating possibility of true
freedom after so long in prison.

I went from one displaced person camp to another in an
effort to find more surviving relatives. Though I was
disappointed again and again, I was compelled to continue
my search.

In my wanderings, I came to Landsberg, a huge German
army camp that became an especially vibrant DP camp,

consisting of Jews who, like me, found themselves without much family or home. This place had an air of excitement about it. On the one hand, everyone there had suffered and lost everything. On the other hand, the energy of choosing a new life and new paths galvanized the place. People stayed up late, talking about various possibilities and planning for the future. I was thrilled to find such a place and such people.

Some people at Landsberg were planning to go to Israel, and form a kibbutz. I could barely contain my enthusiasm; I desperately wanted to go and do my part to claim a homeland for the Jewish people. "Count me in," I told one of the people organizing the effort. And he put my name on the list.

CHAPTER SIXTEEN

FOUND AND LOST

I journeyed back to Feldafing for Sarah, and brought her to Landsberg with me. We moved into a unit on the top floor of one of the buildings. I continued to join in the late night discussions and plans for Israel. Sarah, however, usually stayed in the room. She was shy and spent much of her time staring out the window at goodness knows what. But I decided to let her be. Each of us had to work out the pain of our experiences in his or her own way.

Then one day, Sarah met Sam, the movie-star handsome young man who lived on the floor below ours. Suddenly, my quiet and normally timid sister was a circus act. I can't really blame her. What did we know about dating or courtship with no family or community to model such things before us?

In order to see Sam, Sarah would turn off the water to our floor so that the sinks, showers and toilets couldn't operate. Then my smitten sister would run down to the second floor, buckets in hand, to bring water back to us. This errand took her past Sam's door, where he sometimes stood in the hall. Quite often, she would fill the buckets, carry them upstairs, and then "accidentally" spill them. Down again she went, hoping to catch a second glimpse of Sam. In the meantime, the whole floor had no water. It would have been

aggravating if not for the wonder of being able to laugh at
something again. The rest of us would sit on the stairs
laughing as Sarah *schlepped* buckets of water.

Finally, Sam and Sarah moved past their awkwardness, and he
asked her to marry him. Their wedding was right out of *Fiddler
on the Roof*. What a joyful time. Sarah did the traditional seven
rotations around Sam. They said their vows under the *chuppah*
(the traditional Jewish wedding canopy), broke the glass under
Sam's heel and everyone seemed so happy.

Within the year, they had a daughter named Mary. She
was the most beautiful baby I'd ever seen. To many of us,
she represented the first pure hope and life that managed to
emerge from the ashes of what we had endured. I adored
her. "You know I'm going to totally spoil her," I said to Sarah.

"Rose, you'd better not. She'll need discipline too." I
wouldn't hear of it. Jewish children were never again to be
spanked or punished in any way as far as I was concerned.

As for me, I moved in with the people who were forming
the kibbutz. I had a boyfriend of my own who was also
planning to go to Israel. We were thrilled when the orders
came telling us to prepare to leave.

Sarah invited me to her house for dinner with Sam and
Mary. It was a chance to spend time together before I was
to leave. She eventually persuaded me to stretch my visit to
almost three days.

When I finally returned to the rooms where we kibbutz
members lived, they were empty. Everyone was gone. They
had all left for Israel without me. That's how things
happened in those days, in those places. Permission or
passes came, you packed your few belongings into a shabby
bag, said a few good-byes and left for a new world.

Perhaps I hadn't mentioned to anyone I was going to visit
Sarah. At Landsberg, there was so much mobility, so little
attachment to a "home" and so little family, people just up
and left. They seized the moment, and those left behind
wished them well.

So there I was, staring at empty rooms, deeply disappointed and utterly alone. And angry. I needed to lash out at someone for ruining my plans, and irrationally, that "someone" became Sarah.

"If Sarah hadn't invited me ... if I hadn't stayed so long ..." In my mind, Sarah had spoiled it all. Sarah, basking in her happiness, her husband and her child, had caused my misfortune. Even more irrational was the way in which I decided to "get back" at her.

A man named Leon lived nearby and he was always after me to marry him. Until then I'd only laughed about it. He was a good bit older than me, and I was really too young and inexperienced to contemplate marriage.

Sarah didn't like Leon and I knew that if I were to get involved with him, it would infuriate her. I took a special pleasure in informing her that I'd accepted his proposal.

"Rose, please," she nearly shouted. "You can't marry him!"

"Who are you to tell me what I can and can't do?" I shouted back. "You're not my mother!" I knew that remark would sting her, but I was so frustrated with her and her perfect husband and her perfect child and her thinking that having those things made her qualified to boss me around. "I'm the one who took care of you!" I wanted to say to her, but refrained. Still, the more she tried to dissuade me, the more I fought her.

The wedding was performed at my auntie's. Sarah and one of my cousins accompanied me under the *chuppah*. Even that day, Sarah pulled me aside before the ceremony and pleaded with me to not go through with the marriage. I stubbornly ignored her.

After the wedding, we returned to Landsberg and Leon's apartment. That night, when he came into my bed, I ran out of the room.

"What are you doing?" I cried.

He tried to explain that married couples were supposed to sleep together. But I insisted that I didn't sleep with men.

I had no idea what marriage entailed. I knew nothing about sex. How could I? I hadn't even had my period yet. Years of sadistic and indiscriminate violence had short-circuited the caring formation of my adulthood that the women of my family would have guided.

Not knowing what to do, I ran to Sarah's house. When she explained that it was a wife's obligation—spelled out in the Torah—to sleep with her husband, I thought, "She really is my enemy! How could she tell me to do such a thing?"

Leon found me at Sarah's, and not wanting to be with her anymore, I went with him. I was confused and depressed. Finally, I submitted to his sexual advances. I was so naive and inexperienced that even while we were having sex, I didn't realize it.

One day, as I was standing in line at the movies, I felt a terrible cramp in my stomach. I ran to the bathroom. Looking into the bowl, I saw blood. Thinking I'd cut myself, I cleaned myself up, and went to my sister's house. She explained that I had begun to menstruate.

Soon after that I became pregnant and gave birth to a beautiful son. I cared for him with all the fierceness of first motherhood. My love for him surpassed all my prior understanding of love. I cannot explain the overwhelming feeling of fullness. For the first time in my life I had something entirely my own. I named him Meyer, for my father and somehow, when I held him, I almost felt like my father was with me again.

My joy in my child was tempered by Sarah's announcement that she and Sam and Mary were going to move to Israel. I was both grieved at the thought of her leaving me virtually alone with nobody but my son and a husband I did not love, and envious of her getting to go to the land that had held so many dreams for me. I had wanted to fight for a Jewish homeland—to be part of whatever glories or tribulations were in store for my people.

"Can't we go, too?" I asked Leon. But as it turned out, Leon had other plans. He decided that we were going to America. He never asked me if I wanted to go. "Why America?" I wanted to know.

"We can get a divorce there," he replied. I had no idea about such things, though I knew that as Jews we couldn't apply for a divorce in Germany. Our situation had deteriorated rapidly and we were really husband and wife in name only. I felt nothing for Leon. In the end, I had no choice but to go with him to America. I had no family around to advise me otherwise, so we packed our things and left. Before I knew it, the three of us were on a ship bound for a place called New York.

CHAPTER SEVENTEEN

A NEW COUNTRY

On May 4, 1950, we landed in New York, and were processed and shunted to Philadelphia. It turned out that Leon had family there, a fact he had never mentioned to me. When I met them, they were very reserved toward me. I spoke no English and couldn't communicate with them, and I had no idea what Leon had told them about me. Still, they seemed like a nice Jewish family and even though I was an outsider, I thought I could trust them.

Leon filed for a divorce almost immediately and moved out of the apartment to which we'd been assigned. The first month's rent was free, but after that I was in desperate need of work.

Leon explained that his family could take care of my baby until I got a job, learned English and got more "Americanized." And so they took Meyer to their house. I couldn't think of another option; how could I care for my son without money? I would get a job quickly and then bring him back to live with me.

But when I went to see my baby, Leon's family gave me a very hard time. They wouldn't leave me alone with him, or let me take a walk, or even move freely around their house carrying my child.

One day, fed up, I grabbed my son, and ran back to the apartment. Someone who had befriended me in the neighborhood told me about a Jewish organization that might help me. They would put my son in a foster home, so

I could go to work and I would pay them, just as one would a babysitter. That sounded good to me. I would have more time with my son, and more control over my own life. These plans gave me a spirit of hope.

But as soon as Leon heard what I had done he took me to court. That's when I found out that he had plans to remarry immediately after our divorce was finalized. In fact, his family facilitated these arrangements.

Sitting in court, I didn't understand one word of what was being said. I had no interpreter and no lawyer. That would be an intolerable, if not illegal, judicial situation today. Then, I didn't think it was out of the ordinary; what did I know of the law? Leon was my only link to what was happening. I could only assume he was acting in the best interests of our child.

Things happened fast. The judge looked at me, a woman who lived alone, worked all night in a restaurant where I'd finally managed to find a job cooking and cleaning—anything to pay the rent. Then he looked at Leon and his new woman. She had a house, and to the courts, being a property owner implied stability.

The court awarded Leon custody of Meyer. Just like that, the judge banged his gavel, and someone explained to me that Meyer would live with Leon from now on. I think I passed out for a moment and then I started crying hysterically, and had to be escorted from the courtroom.

I felt ripped open and despair began to fill the hole in my heart. I felt like I was dying. If I'd had a gun at that moment, I think I would have killed Leon and then myself. I hated him for what he'd done to me; how he'd used me.

Leon eventually confessed to me that he was already engaged to this woman while we were still in Germany. I was astounded.

"Why on earth did you marry me then?" I confronted him.

"I needed to get to America. I knew I'd have a better chance of getting permission to enter the country if I was married."

I was speechless for a moment. Then I said, "And how could you just take away my child like that? I mean nothing to you. You're a monster."

He looked at me and said calmly, "He's the only son I'll ever have." I learned then that his wife could not have children.

I was allowed to visit Meyer in their home. I always looked at Leon's new wife with a contempt I'm now ashamed of. She and Leon had stolen the only thing in life that mattered to me. A few months later, they moved from Philadelphia to somewhere in New Jersey. Before it was difficult to see my son, but once they moved, I didn't see him at all. The pain of losing Meyer rivaled everything I had suffered in the camps. It was almost too much to bear.

I gave up the apartment Leon and I had shared for the briefest of times and began renting a room in a house owned by a family in West Philadelphia, in a neighborhood called Strawberry Mansion. The rent was cheaper and the people were nice to me. And I liked the area. It was the kind of place where after school, children stopped at the candy and cigar shop on the corner, clutching their pennies as they eyed the bright sweets behind the glass counters. Two bakeries, including one that sold fresh *challah* bread, were within easy walking distance, along with two butcher shops and a grocery store. Clothing shops, shoe stores and hardware stores were also right nearby. So were bus stops, providing easy access to trolleys and the elevated trains that I could take downtown.

To lessen my loneliness, I began to explore the city more. To me, downtown Philadelphia was a magical place. I loved simply walking along Chestnut Street and Walnut Street. The lights, the tall buildings, the elegant stores and theaters, the clubs and restaurants all sparkled into a goblet I had never had a chance to taste.

I got a job closer to my new residence, working at the counter of a small restaurant. One frosty winter day a handsome fellow came in. I had recently become interested in movies and the like, and I thought he looked like a cross between James Cagney and Edward G. Robinson. He took a menu, and pretended to study it, but I could tell that actually, he was "looking me over", as we would have said back in Skarzysko. When he said, "This, I'll have to get some," I didn't know whether he was referring to the food or to me.

He ordered a steak, and told me how he wanted it cooked. After I prepared it, I placed it in front of him. He smiled at me and picked up his knife and fork. With every bite of meat, he repeated, "Oy! This is the best steak I ever ate."

My boss sat down next to him at the counter, and said, "Charlie, the way you're enjoying that steak, it's worth at least a five dollar tip." Charlie smiled, reached into his pocket, pulled out a five-dollar bill, and laid it on the counter. Without blinking an eye, I reached down and scooped it up. At that time, five dollars was a fortune!

Charlie returned to the restaurant the next day and the day after and the day after that. A few weeks after his first visit, he came over just before closing time, looking more dressed up (and more nervous) than usual. His trousers were creased to a knife-edge and his white shirt was starched within an inch of its life. He didn't sit down; he just looked at me for a moment before he asked, "Rose, may I take you to dinner?"

I was pleased at his invitation, but trying to be coy, I told him, "I'm sorry, Charlie, I already have a date." I was dressed to go downtown from work, wearing a V-neck black cocktail dress and high-heeled fancy French shoes, which were open-toed and made of clear plastic. I was attired as stylishly as I knew how.

When I said I had a date, Charlie simply nodded. The silence between us mirrored the silence of the snow falling outside; the electricity between us contrasted with the quiet stillness of the night.

Charlie looked toward the window: "It's really coming down out there."

I nodded, gazing at the three inches of snow that had already accumulated on the ground. I cleared my throat. "Well," I began, "I really should get going. Would you mind giving me a ride to the subway station?"

"Sure," he said.

My toes tingled as we walked through the snow to his car. When we got in, though, his car refused to start. "Oh no," Charlie said, "I forgot to put in, you know, the winter stuff."

"Winter stuff?"

"Yes, the . . . the . . . antifreeze," he said, snapping his fingers when he came upon the right word.

"Antifreeze," I repeated.

"Look," he said, "I could get a friend to drive us to the station and drop you off for your big date or if you are hungry, we can stop in a restaurant and have dinner and wait until the weather lets up. Then if you like, I can still get you to the station."

I never made it downtown that night. The snow was falling heavier as Charlie and I sat down to dinner in a small cozy restaurant near where I lived. We were the only customers in the place. As we lingered over our coffee and cake, the owner approached us. "Either of you two know anything about restaurants?"

"I work in one," I responded.

"Good," he said. "The weather is so lousy, I'm going to go in the back and take a nap. If, by some miracle, any customers should happen to come in, let me know. Otherwise, you can let yourselves out. No charge for the meal." And with that, he disappeared to the back of the restaurant.

Charlie and I sat across from each other in a booth and talked all night. Periodically, I got up to make more coffee and fill our cups. Sitting there, in the booth with him, it was the first time in my life I'd truly felt like a woman. I was able to talk to him about things I'd never shared with a man before—things that had happened to me. I didn't go into too many details about my years in the concentration camps, but he'd been in the Army and could fill in some of the gaps I left blank. I thought my past might frighten him, but something in the earnestness of his eyes made me feel as though I could trust him, and so I shared from my heart.

It was exhilarating to be able to confide in someone after all this time. As it grew lighter and lighter outside, and the sun's rays began to make the snow glisten, I knew, as certain as the dawn comes after dark, that I was going to spend the rest of my life with Charlie.

CHAPTER EIGHTEEN

A NEW FAMILY

"Rose, where have you been?" The landlady's voice startled me as I tried to stealthily enter the house the morning after my night in the restaurant with Charlie. "I was so worried," she continued, "what with the storm and all . . ."

"I'm fine," I assured her, and the look on my face must have told her that "fine" was an incredible understatement. I began to hum as I walked down the hall to my room, and she came after me. "You didn't!"

"Didn't what?" I asked, startled.

"Rose, did you get married last night?"

"What are you talking about?" I stammered incredulously.

"Well, why are you humming the wedding march?" she asked bluntly.

"Was I?" I asked, feeling the heat rise in my cheeks.

"You certainly were! I thought, 'She's gone and gotten married.'"

I smiled. "I haven't gotten married, Ruth." Satisfied that her suspicions were unfounded, she turned and left. I fell into bed and into a deep, contented sleep.

"Rose?" I heard knocking on my door and my landlady's voice on the other side. "Yes?" I mumbled, looking around, trying to gauge how long I'd slept. Judging from the light outside, it must have been a few hours. I got up from my bed and went to open the door. "What is it?"

"There's something in the kitchen you should see."

I followed her and my eyes fell on a big bag of cakes and bagels. Beside the bag was a flower with a card attached that said "Rose."

My landlady eyed my pleased expression with amusement. "It was on the porch when I went to get the paper," she explained. "Now, Rose, is there something you'd like to tell us?"

We sat down to enjoy some pastries and hot coffee, and I answered their inquiries as delicately as I could manage. When the phone rang, I almost leapt for it but decided to let the landlady take the call. Just as I suspected, it was Charlie.

"The snow has let up. I'm coming to get you," he said decisively.

We picked up where we'd left off the night before, talking all night in a quiet restaurant. It was a simple, magical evening, the kind of night when the ordinary becomes extraordinary, the simple things become significant, when words are not always necessary and everything just seems to glow in the mysterious radiance of love being born.

The following weekend, Charlie took me to meet his parents in Brooklyn. As we drove up he sang love songs to me in his deep, strong voice. When we got to his parents' house, I looked around, trying to discover new things about Charlie's background that would either signal confirmation or warning. But the house seemed cozy and normal.

When Charlie introduced me to his parents, his father asked him in Yiddish, "Is this the same one from two weeks ago, Charlie?"

I immediately answered for him, "Nein!" Realizing I understood Yiddish, they laughed, and our closeness was sealed from then on.

We eloped soon after and found a home at the end of a block of row houses. Each house had a small yard in the front and a slightly larger one in the back. The neighborhood was mostly Jewish, though most of the residents had become very "Americanized."

I began life with a man who was gentle, kind and loving and who made me feel like he couldn't have done better than to find me as a wife. Most endearing was his sense of humor. He could always make me laugh; even in the midst of an argument he would crack a joke and calm the waters. He loved to tell jokes. Unfortunately he often laughed so hard at his own jokes that the punch lines were rarely reached, leaving us frustrated. But his laugh was so infectious, we couldn't help but laugh with him.

Not that we didn't have our problems from time to time. For instance, because of my upbringing, I wanted to keep a kosher home, but Charlie, who wasn't religious at all, couldn't see the sense of using different dishes for different meals. He did attempt to adjust, but in the end, he broke so many dishes while washing or stacking them that I eventually gave up; I couldn't keep replacing dishes, so I let him have his way. Besides, I only wanted to keep kosher for tradition's sake, not because I had any real love for God.

The most wonderful thing Charlie did was insist on trying to find my son, Meyer. In those days it wasn't as easy to track people down as it is today. All I knew was that Leon had moved to New Jersey. I didn't have an address or phone number. We looked through telephone directories but we never found him listed. Every time we'd cross the Delaware River into New Jersey, we'd stop in cities or towns we hadn't explored to see if anyone knew him. But no luck. Leon hadn't committed a crime, so we couldn't go to the police. As time went on and we still couldn't find him, we began to lose hope that I'd ever be reunited with my son.

Charlie and I had three beautiful children of our own. First came Norman, our son, then Miriam, whom we affectionately call Cookie, and then Candy. She was born three months prematurely, and for years we didn't know if

she would live or die. I was always gentler with her than
with the other two, who caused me much more *tsuris*
(trouble) in return. For instance, I didn't know it, but when
Candy was little, Norman and Miriam told her she was
adopted. They also told her that if she ever asked me about
it, I would send her back to the orphanage. Perhaps that's
why she was so well behaved. Anyway, when she finally
realized it was a hoax, she didn't forgive them for years.

But other than those kinds of squabbles, the three
children lived relatively uncomplicated lives. They went to
public schools and when they were the right age, they all
attended Hebrew school and became *bar* and *bat mitzvah*.
We lived across the street from the synagogue, so it was
very convenient.

I kept myself quite busy with synagogue and other Jewish
activities. We celebrated all the festivals. I worked tirelessly
for every Jewish organization that would have me and that I
enjoyed. I even became president of the synagogue at one
point. But I never had any real time for God. And I certainly
felt no affection or love for him. I loved being with my
people and working for Jewish causes, but as far as I was
concerned, a loving God wouldn't have allowed the pain
and misery I and my family and millions of others had
endured. "How could a loving God let so many of us suffer
like that?" was my constant question. And there was never
an answer good enough to make me believe again.

CHAPTER NINETEEN

BETRAYAL

When Cookie was old enough, I sometimes sent her outside to clear the snow from the walk. Rarely did she have to attend to this task herself, however, because as soon as she went out the door, the boys of the neighborhood swarmed around her. It was like she was the queen bee and they were worker bees. There was no shortage of volunteers to shovel the sidewalk for her. Such were the amusements of having a teenage daughter.

Around that time, Cookie began to disappear for a few hours each day. I figured she was hanging out with friends of hers and didn't pay too much mind. I noticed that when she got home, she'd often be humming and singing songs I'd never heard before. As her mother, I was just glad she seemed so happy.

But then one day she came home and her face was lit up and she looked more ecstatic than I'd ever seen her. I figured maybe she'd met a boy she liked but as it turns out, I was way off the mark.

"Mommy, I believe in Jesus Christ! He's the Jewish Messiah!"

If she'd opened her jacket, pulled out a gun and shot me, it would have been better than hearing those words.

"Miriam, what are you talking about?" I demanded. "Where did you hear such things?"

"From the Bible studies I've been going to with my friends."

"The what?!" I screamed at her. "You're Jewish; you don't go to those things!"

Realizing that my daughter had been hanging around with "them" all this time and I hadn't known about it—and that she'd come to believe in our worst enemy—it was too much. I completely lost my composure.

"I'd rather you'd become a whore!" I screamed at her.

Scared and confused, Miriam ran upstairs to her room and shut the door. I could scarcely believe the rage that boiled inside me. I went up the stairs after her, but couldn't bring myself to face her. So I went back downstairs. Then up again. Then down. After four or five trips up and down the stairs, I felt I was calm enough to actually enter her room.

I walked in and sat down on the bed where she was laying. "Miriam," I began, "Do you realize why you don't have grandparents or aunts or uncles or cousins who come over and give you candy and presents and celebrate the holidays with you like some of your friends have? Do you realize that once, I did have those things? I had a mother and a bubbe and a zayde and so many others and now they are all gone." My voice started to quake a bit, "Miriam, you have no idea the things we suffered, the things that were taken away from us . . . and all because of him." I couldn't bring myself to say the name. "Every time they beat us or tortured us or killed us, it was because of him."

"But Mommy," Miriam replied, "It wasn't the Jesus of the Bible who did those things . . ." When she said his name I wanted to smash my fist into her face. To me, it was a curse word. "Don't speak of him again!" I cried. There is an old Jewish tradition that says that "a table should not be ashamed" by not having people at it. "He has shamed my table! He took away my family!"

"But Mommy . . ."

"No!" I yelled. "You cannot believe in him. I forbid it! You could not have hurt me more than you have right now, do you understand? You have three days. Three days, to choose whether you want to believe this trash or leave the house. Because I will not have that name uttered here again!" I slammed the door behind me so hard I thought the walls would crack.

Three days later, Miriam had made her choice. "I still believe in him, Mommy"

"Then get out," I told her. With tears in her eyes, she packed some of her belongings and left.

CHAPTER TWENTY

THE HOUSE OF THE DEAD

As soon as Miriam left, I did what any sensible Jewish mother would do: I followed her. As angry and hurt as I was, I loved her desperately and feared for her all the more. I had to know where she was going.

She ended up at a house not too far away from where we lived. On the lawn in front of the house sat a group of young people. A few of them had guitars or small percussion instruments. As they played, the rest of the group sang songs that I figured were the ones Miriam had been singing at home. My heart sank as I looked at this raggedy assembly. Most of them had straggly long hair and sported torn jeans as a badge of honor. They all looked as though they could use a good scrubbing. As I ran home, my imagination ran amuck. By the time I reached my husband, I was out of breath.

"Charlie, do you know what kind of crowd our daughter is running with? She's hooked up with those Jesus freaks!"

"Calm down, Rose," he said, adding, "Come on, it could be worse."

"How could it be worse!" I yelled at him. "We have no idea what these kids are up to." In my mind, I'd already pictured them having sex orgies regularly, using various psychedelic drugs and goodness knows what else.

113

I decided to go to the District Attorney's office, where I met with Arlen Spector, hoping to get that house broken up somehow. But he said there was nothing that he could do. "We keep an eye on that house," he tried to reassure me, but I was far from consoled.

I returned home, which seemed to have become a battlefield almost overnight. When I tried to talk to Charlie about Miriam, he said I was getting hysterical, which I was. Candy, who was still in Hebrew school, grew sullen. "It's your fault my sister is gone," she said to me. "Hey, you and your sister used to do little else than fight," I told her. But I missed Miriam, too. And I was scared.

One day as I was cleaning Miriam's room, I saw a piece of cloth poking out from under her bed. I pulled at it. It was the shirt she'd just "had to have" because "all the girls in school have one." I remembered how I'd indulged her, thinking, "My child shouldn't want for anything. She should have everything I never had and then some." Seeing that blouse seared my heart afresh.

I went downstairs and approached Charlie, who was reading a newspaper. In as calm a tone as I could muster, I simply said almost in a whisper, "Please, honey, please just go check on her. Just drive by and see if you see her . . . or if you can, talk to her. I just want to know that she's all right. I mean . . ." My words faltered.

So Charlie drove over to the house. He was gone for hours. I nearly worried myself sick while he was gone. When he returned, it was all I could do to keep from pouncing on him.

"What happened?" I asked.

"Well," he began, "When I got there, I walked in, looking for Miriam. And I saw these kids on the floor. They were just sitting on the floor, and I realized they were praying . . ."

I began to feel a lump in my throat. The lump grew bigger as Charlie continued to tell me what had happened, that he was moved by the sight of teenagers openly and passionately praying. When they invited him to sit down with them, he did. Then he said, "Rose, I believe Jesus is the Messiah."

I couldn't speak at first. Then I said, "I don't get it, Charlie. I have to practically beg you to come to synagogue with me. And when you do, you don't even stay for the whole time. You don't even care about God, let alone a Messiah!"

"You're right. Yesterday I didn't care. But it's true, Rose. Here let me show you ..." He went to pick up a Bible he'd set on a table. I grabbed it first.

"No! It's one thing for Miriam to believe this garbage; she's just a child. But for you to do this to me ..." I took the Bible and hurled it at him as hard as I could. It struck him right in the face.

I froze. In all our years of marriage, we'd never raised a hand to one another. I could barely look at Charlie. A fierce look rose into his eyes, and I turned and stumbled toward the door, frightened of what he might do. I opened the door and ran out of the house, and I stayed away for at least two hours. Eventually I knew I had to go back and face him.

I was petrified as I opened the door and walked back into the house. Charlie was pretty much where I'd left him, but the anger had drained from his expression. He looked up at me and said quietly, "I want Miriam to come home." I knew better than to argue with him at this time.

So she moved back home, and it began to feel as though my whole family had turned against me. I found out that even my sweet Candy had "accepted the Lord." When I heard this I stormed into Miriam's room. "Your father and I work hard so that your sister can go to Hebrew school and you feed her these lies!" Then in a blind rage I hit her. I hit her so hard she bruised. The next day when I saw the bruises, I couldn't believe it. "Who did this to you?" I demanded to know.

"You did, Mommy," she said softly. "It was you."

I couldn't believe it. I didn't even remember doing it.

After that I felt guilty, and I knew we had to establish some semblance of a truce if this family were to survive. Besides, I began to have a glimmer of hope that maybe all of this was just a phase; that they'd all snap out of it and we'd be happy again.

I tried to lay down some ground rules: no praying in the house, no reading the Bible and no gathering of those "freaks" in my house. The daily ritual was set up. In the morning, after the children left for school, I went upstairs to straighten their bedrooms. If I found a Bible, I opened the back windows overlooking the alley and threw it and any other Jesus paraphernalia into the garbage cans below. When the kids returned from school, the first thing they did was rummage through the cans to retrieve their Bibles. Sometimes the garbage man came first, so I vividly remember Charlie chasing the garbage truck down the street, yelling after the garbage man to stop so he could find their Bibles.

Oh Charlie. I loved him so much, and yet I felt so betrayed by him that for the most part, I stopped speaking to him. I felt I could no longer go to him with my grief; he didn't understand me anymore. It got so bad that I could barely look at him.

The children wisely steered clear of their parents' problems. And I began to notice a change in them. They became more helpful around the house, tidying up, doing the dishes, picking up after themselves. I said nothing. If this was part of their newfound faith, it was the one part I was willing to accept.

The situation at home was so bad, I began looking for a way out. I went to a lawyer. I explained what was happening and told him I wanted to leave my house and my family. He convinced me that legally I didn't have the grounds and that I might be guilty of desertion. "That's a laugh," I thought, "Considering they are the ones who've deserted me."

I knew I couldn't leave my family, but I still needed someone who would talk to me and understand me. I decided to go to my rabbi. When I explained the situation, he looked at me and said matter-of-factly, "I hate to tell you this, Rose, but you are living in "the house of the dead." Paradoxically, I found myself in a position where I felt I had to defend the family I had just vilified. "I don't understand," I said. "They can't be dead. There must be something I can do."

"I'm sure you'll come to understand what I mean, Rose. Your family have turned their back on their faith. They are apostates. Until then, you would do well to study the Scriptures. I'm sure they are about to come after you to try and convince you of what they believe." Before I left, he handed me a Bible. I thanked him and left, feeling no better than when I'd first arrived.

CHAPTER TWENTY-ONE

THE BASEMENT

Where I grew up in Poland, women didn't read the Scriptures for themselves; that kind of study was the men's responsibility. So I was ill prepared when, true to the rabbi's warning, my children started leaving me little bits of paper with Scripture references written on them. In fact, at first I didn't realize what the "Gen." and "Ps." and "Is." meant. But it didn't matter; I threw the pieces of paper away.

Then they took the Bible the rabbi had given me and they underlined these Scripture passages and tabbed them with pieces of paper. When I saw it, I was enraged. I ran across the street to the rabbi and threw the Bible on his desk. "Look what they've done! They've defaced the Scriptures! Why do they want me to read these things?"

The rabbi sighed with disdain. "They think that if you read these verses, then you will be convinced that they point to Jesus as the Messiah, but for every one of these 'proofs' I can give you two other verses to counter it."

I found a good deal of pleasure in going back to my children and showing them the verses that the rabbi had come up with. I barely knew anything about the Bible, but I began a sort of chess match with my children. I showed them the rabbis' verses, then they took those verses to Joe Finkelstein, the owner of the house my Miriam had lived in, and he gave them more verses to answer the rabbi. The exchanges continued, and I was only just beginning to understand that the Torah and the Prophets contain a plan

that God has for his people, including his promise that one
day a Messiah would come to deliver his people.

I'd heard of the Messiah. I knew that before he came,
Moses and Elijah would come first, or so the rabbis said. I
knew that he was supposed to establish peace on earth. But
I didn't know just how much else the *Tanakh* had to say
about him.

One day, the children showed me Isaiah 53, which reads.

Who has believed our report? And to whom has the arm of
the LORD been revealed? For He shall grow up before Him as a
tender plant, and as a root out of dry ground. He has no form or
comeliness; and when we see Him, there is no beauty that we
should desire him. He is despised and rejected by men, a Man of
sorrows and acquainted with grief. And we hid, as it were, our
faces from Him; He was despised, and we did not esteem Him.

Surely He has borne our griefs and carried our sorrows;
yet we esteemed Him stricken, smitten by God, and afflicted.
But He was wounded for our transgressions, He was bruised
for our iniquities; the chastisement for our peace was upon
Him, and by His stripes we are healed. All we like sheep
have gone astray; we have turned, every one, to his own
way; and the LORD has laid on Him the iniquity of us all.

He was oppressed and He was afflicted, yet He opened
not His mouth; He was led as a lamb to the slaughter, and as
a sheep before its shearers is silent, so He opened not His
mouth. He was taken from prison and from judgment, and
who will declare His generation? For He was cut off from
the land of the living; for the transgressions of My people He
was stricken. And they made His grave with the wicked—
but with the rich at His death, because He had done no
violence, nor was any deceit in His mouth.

Yet it pleased the LORD to bruise Him; He has put Him to
grief. When You make His soul an offering for sin, He shall
see His seed, He shall prolong His days, and the pleasure of
the LORD shall prosper in His hand.

He shall see of the labor of His soul, and be satisfied. By His knowledge My righteous servant shall justify many, for He shall bear their iniquities. Therefore I will divide Him a portion with the great, and He shall divide the spoil with the strong, because He poured out His soul unto death, and He was numbered with the transgressors, and He bore the sin of many, and made intercession for the transgressors.

It was enough to make me do a double-take before I ran to my rabbi with it. When I handed it to him, he said to me sternly and sadly, "You are one of them."

"No I'm not!" I said. "I just want to know what it really means. Is it about the Messiah? Help me."

He sighed. "It's King David," he said, "Just like in Psalm 22 and so many of the other passages that your family wants to distort."

But he seemed exasperated and would have no more discussion with me about it. So I went home, confused and a bit angry. I grabbed Cookie's Bible and my Bible, went down to the basement and locked myself in the bathroom with just the Bibles and the telephone. I started comparing the two versions of the Bible and the passages the kids had underlined. There was little difference between Cookie's Bible and my own.

I turned once again to Isaiah 53. My eyes fell on verse 10: "Yet it pleased the Lord to bruise him ..." Who was "him"? Could it really have been David, as the rabbi said? But how did David bear the "sin of many"?

I still needed some answers, and since the rabbi seemed more aloof, I didn't know where to go. Then I remembered that we lived near a seminary where the "goyim" studied. "Maybe they could help me understand," I thought.

Never in my life had I stepped into St. Charles Seminary, a Catholic seminary, no less. I went upstairs and out the door and into the summer heat. I perspired as I walked and each footstep seemed to echo the words, "It can't be him, it can't be him ..." I finally reached the seminary, hot and weary from walking. Yet at first, I could not bring myself to cross the threshold.

I took a deep breath and opened the door. Cool air greeted me, but did nothing to calm me down. I walked into the office. A man came toward me. Shaking, I held out my Bible, opened to Isaiah 53. "What does this mean?" I demanded, pointing to verse 10.

"It pleased God to bruise him," he said.

"I know what it says! But what does it mean?"

"It's talking about Jesus. It means that it pleased God to bruise Jesus for our sins."

"Oh is that so? If it pleased God to bruise him, then why did you put me and my family in a concentration camp! I didn't kill him!" I shouted, almost crying at the same time.

The man sat down on one of the couches in the waiting area, bowed his head and said, "I'm sorry, I'm so sorry. I'm so sorry we did that to you."

I'd never heard an apology for what had happened to me in the camps, let alone from a Christian. His humility disarmed me somewhat, and I apologized for venting my anger on him. And then I stood there, not knowing what else to say or do, not even knowing how I'd gotten there, really.

Someone from the seminary drove me home. The next day I went back down to the basement. I had Cookie's Bible with me and began to read the gospel of Matthew. It begins with the genealogy of Jesus. I saw names I knew: King David, Abraham, Isaac, Jacob. I felt as though Matthew was saying to me, "See Rose? He's Jewish."

I read through the gospel to see where exactly Jesus becomes our enemy. In the back of my mind were echoes of guards shouting at me, "Christ-killer! Jesus hates you, you swine!"

But the Jesus in the pages in front of me was not hateful. He was loving and kind and compassionate. He wasn't a lion; he was a lamb. And oh, how he suffered. I knew that he would be able to understand my pain. I knew there was no way he could be in Nazi uniform, beating and cursing me. It was far easier to see him in the clothes of a prisoner, suffering beside me. "He doesn't hate me," I thought. "It wasn't his fault."

I stayed down in the basement for hours, days, reading more and more of my daughter's New Testament. I devoured it ravenously and time slipped by without my knowledge. When I emerged from downstairs, I had a new understanding of Jesus, but I was far from believing him to be the Messiah. I had seen too much to believe that his coming had accomplished anything; certainly not the peace on earth we were awaiting.

I began to permit more of my daughters' friends to come over to the house, though I still didn't trust them. As the High Holidays approached, I prepared for them with a certain rigor that was my way of saying, "See, I'm Jewish. You're not."

But just before Rosh Hashanah, Charlie had a heart attack. I was bewildered and scared. The world was coming off its axis. I couldn't drive, so Miriam arranged for some of her friends to take me to the hospital.

When they let me into Charlie's room, he was conscious and his condition seemed stable. I sat beside his bed all day. Every so often he pleaded with me in a weakened voice, "Rose, please, please say yes to Jesus. Please." I didn't want to upset him, but I couldn't do what he asked. "Charlie, I know that Jesus wasn't the hateful person I thought he was, but he's not God. He's a man and I can't pray to a man." He fell asleep with a sad expression on his face.

The next day was Erev Rosh Hashanah. I went to visit Charlie as soon as visiting hours permitted. Charlie's doctor was in the room when I entered. "Rose, just do whatever it is he wants you to do. Don't stress him." I wanted to say, "You have no idea what he's asking of me." But I refrained. I went over to Charlie. "Hi there," I said softly. He removed his oxygen mask and looked at me. "Rose, I want you to go to the prayer meeting with Miriam tonight."

"You want me to go there tonight? On Rosh Hashanah?"

I asked, still trying to keep calm. "Yes," he replied with not a little effort. "Go tonight."

Remembering what the doctor said, I nodded, and left. When I got home, I went across the street to the synagogue and asked the rabbi to pray for my husband's recovery.

He shook his head. "No, your husband is already dead."

Had I heard correctly? On the eve of Rosh Hashanah, my rabbi was refusing to pray for my husband. My Charlie was recovering from a heart attack and my rabbi wouldn't pray for him? Even people standing around us began to argue with him. "Her husband isn't asking you," they said. "Rose, Rose who's worked for years for our synagogue is asking."

He still refused. I ran out, swearing I wouldn't return for Rosh Hashanah services. I crossed the street again. The divide between my house and the synagogue had just become a chasm.

Miriam and some of her friends were waiting for me at the house. They begged me to get dressed and come to a new congregation they were attending.

I was too tired to fight. On the eve of this Rosh Hashanah, my soul yearned to be with my people, to pray with my people. I thought of my family, long dead, and I urgently felt the need to say Kaddish, the prayer praising God said in remembrance of loved ones and others who have died. It was not enough for me to say it in my house. God urges a sacred assembly on Shabbat and other festivals. I needed to say Kaddish among my people.

So I went with my daughter and her friends to Ed Brupsky's Messianic congregation in the area. I didn't even know what a "Messianic" congregation was.

As soon as the leader, Ed Brupsky, saw me come in with my daughter, he said, "Let's pray for our brother, Charlie, who is in the hospital with a heart attack." And all these people began to pray for him, silently and out loud. A feeling of warmth came over me. I'd never felt anything like it.

When the prayers were over, I felt a bit overwhelmed and got up and walked into the next room. A woman followed me and said, "Rose Price?" I turned around. "That's me," I said. She pointed her finger at me and said, "If you're not going to accept Christ, you're going to hell!"

I looked her in the eyes and spat out, "You know what? I've been to hell, and it was people like you who put me there! I'm Jewish. I won't accept your God."

"I'm Jewish too," she replied.

"No, you're not! A Jew wouldn't talk like that. And who made you judge, anyway?"

Somebody must have heard the exchange, and came running to pull me away from her. The children who'd brought me surrounded me protectively, and took me home.

"I swear I'll never go back there," I told them. I wanted nothing to do with that woman and her ilk. At home once again, I roused myself and crossed the street to the synagogue. It was still Rosh Hashanah eve. I walked up the aisle of the synagogue to our seats, Charlie's and mine. Everyone turned to look at me. I suddenly felt as though I was a stranger in my own synagogue. When I saw the rabbi up front at the *bima*, I knew I was still angry. Not wanting to create a scene, I turned around and left.

CHAPTER TWENTY-TWO

SPECIAL INVITATIONS

After five days in the hospital under observation, Charlie was allowed to come home. He seemed as healthy as ever. This was during the Days of Awe, the ten days of repentance between Rosh Hashanah and Yom Kippur, the Day of Atonement. What is normally a somber time was brightened by my husband's return home.

While we were in the midst of celebrating, I heard about a special dinner party being planned at millionaire Arthur DeMoss' residence. The price of admission was to bring a Jewish person who didn't believe in Jesus. Suddenly I felt like I was the most popular person in Philadelphia!

Debbie Finkelstein invited me to be her guest. As curious as I was to "see how the other half lives," I didn't want to go. But Charlie said it would make him very happy if I went. And so I grudgingly obliged. When I accepted Debbie's invitation I said impertinently, "Fine, I'll have dinner at the DeMoss house, and I'll have Jesus Christ for dessert."

When we arrived, Mr. DeMoss, a prominent, respected businessman, greeted us. After we were all seated in his impressive house, he welcomed us as a group and began talking about how "believing in Jesus was a very Jewish thing to do." Only he used the word "Y'shua" instead of Jesus. "Tonight," Mr. DeMoss said, "I hope we'll get a chance

to see how the concept of Messiah is fundamental to
Judaism and how the Torah, the Prophets and the Writings
all show us that Y'shua is our Messiah."

I was ready to choke this man for his obvious objective to
"convert" me. "You aren't Jewish!" I wanted to yell. "What
do you know?"

I managed to stay polite throughout dinner. Afterwards,
we watched a film called "Dry Bones" which was of course
about Jesus. Then Manny Brotman, who was there with his
wife Audrey, both Jewish believers in Jesus, gave a teaching.

I left the room when he started talking and walked into
another where I could be alone. I was pacing back and
forth like a caged animal when Debbie came looking for me,
took me by the arm, and led me to a corner.

"Rose, why don't you pray and ask God if Jesus is really
the Messiah?" I just stared at her. "Debbie, I haven't prayed
to my God since 1941. You think I'm going to pray to *your*
God? You want me to not be Jewish anymore!"

She kept insisting that I wasn't giving up my Judaism.
"You'll understand, Rose. Soon you'll understand."

Arthur DeMoss, seeing us in heated conversation, came
over. "Rose, would you like me to pray with you?"

"I don't pray to your God," I said defiantly.

"Well, do you mind if I pray?"

"It's your house. You can stand on your head if you want."

Mr. DeMoss then bowed his head and began to pray. Many
others came in then and prayed with him. They all closed
their eyes. I kept mine open. I was taught that a Jewish
person never closes his or her eyes while praying. We might
miss something. We want to see if Elijah comes. But I
eventually closed my eyes that night and let these people's
prayers wash over me and bring me peace, just as they had
done at Ed Brupsky's group. At 2:00 in the morning I opened
my eyes. Hours had passed without me realizing it, and I felt
as if gigantic stones had rolled off my back. All the heaviness
in my heart had left me. It was as though I had found a

warm, safe place after being outside in the cold for a long time. And it was in this place where I could finally pray.

"God of Abraham, Isaac and Jacob," I said, "if it's true that he—you know who—is your Son and my Messiah, that's okay. But if he isn't, that's okay too. We haven't talked all these years, but we will still go on being friends." Then I added another prayer quickly: "If it's true that he is the Messiah, then I want him. I will do whatever he wants me to do, and I will go wherever he wants me to go. But please, make me sure that he is."

That was September 21, 1971, appropriately enough, during the Days of Awe. This date is etched in my mind as my day of *t'shuvah*, the day I turned toward God.

Soon after this, I went to the hospital with blood clots in my legs. The doctors decided to operate on the leg to remove a vein. But another clot developed in my lungs. I vaguely remember hearing the doctors discussing a procedure to wall off the lower half of my body so the clots could not come up from my legs. I would be in a wheelchair for the rest, of my life.

I would not accept that. "I do not give you permission to cripple me! I will take your hospital and everything you have!" I remember saying.

They did not operate. I began to feel worse and worse. I remember hearing one of the doctors say, "At least she'll have an easy death. She'll just go in and out of comas that will get deeper and deeper until she passes away."

I began to lose hope. I was existing in a painkiller-induced stupor, and I lost all track of time. And then, one day, I opened my eyes and Charlie was standing at my bedside. There was also a stranger beside him. "You're going to operate on me, aren't you?" I whispered.

"Yes, but only if you'll let me."

"You want to cut me in half?"

He smiled. "No, I won't cut you at all. I'm just going to make a small incision, and insert a small piece, kind of like an umbrella."

I knew I hadn't heard him correctly. "A what?"

"It's experimental," he went on to explain. "We don't know if it's going to work, but I really feel we should try to save your life." That was the last thing I remember before everything faded to black. That was December of 1971. When I awoke, everyone surrounding the bed—Charlie, my children and the doctors—welcomed me into the new year, 1972.

I had survived. I had both my legs. In my heart I knew that God had interceded for me; that he had heard the prayers of my children and my husband and all their friends, and he had responded. From then on, I began to see God as the deliverer; not as a far-off being who just allowed suffering to happen, but as a God who was with me in my suffering and who sustained me through it.

Reliance on God was a hard lesson to learn. For so long I had felt that if I were to survive, let alone be successful, I would have to do so on my own. The idea that I could literally entrust my life to God was a whole new world.

As I recovered my strength, I began to read the Bible constantly. Sometimes I would even forget to cook dinner or clean the house. The kids knew what was happening to me, and from then on those Jesus Freaks would congregate either at my house or what was affectionately known as the Fink Zoo. When they were at my house and my door was closed, they kept very quiet so as not to disturb me. "Rose is studying," they would say to one another.

I like to say now that the Lord and I had a great honeymoon. Those months of study were one long feast. And the more I read, the more convinced I became that Jesus was who he claimed to be. I accepted his death as the atonement for my sins, and because he rose from the dead, I believe he is coming again, to right all the wrongs, to bring peace where there is none, and to take away all the hurt from our hearts.

Yes, I accepted Y'shua, not despite my Jewishness but *because* I am Jewish and he is my Messiah. My Judaism really began to mean so much more to me as I discovered Jesus as the fulfillment of the *Tanakh* and as I invited him to change me, and to make me more like him.

I didn't know it until later, but after I had dinner and prayed at the DeMoss house, Charlie and my children and their friends had gotten a group of people to commit to praying that I would realize that Jesus was true. I've met people here and there since, who were on that "prayer chain." Some of them have said, "You're Rose Price? You were a tough nut to crack!" I always laugh, because I know it's true.

One day not long after I was released from the hospital and recovered my strength, some dear friends of ours— Mennonites who'd prayed for me while I was in the hospital—invited Charlie and me to their church. From the beginning, I hadn't understood why they would pray for me, a Jew, but I accepted it. Now we went to their church as guests, and the pastor invited me to share my testimony with the congregation. I had no idea what he meant. To me, a testimony was something you gave in court. I didn't even know how to hold a mike. I was so confused I thought I would pass out.

Then Charlie said to me, "Rose, just tell them what God has done for you. God gave you a testimony, a story. Now share!"

So I started sharing. The first words out of my mouth must have been garbled, but I continued speaking because these friends loved me, my family, and the Jewish people. Imagine—my Jewish people were loved! In turn, I loved the people of that congregation.

When we got home, Charlie told me that God had used me. I didn't understand. Used me? He used Moses, not me.

"Rose, you have a ministry."

"A what?"

"Yes, I think that you are meant to share your story with others."

That night I went on my face to the Lord, and cried out, "If you want me to share my story, you have to teach me how to do it. Teach me what to say, and how to say it." I don't know how many hours I lay there, but when I got up, I knew, without a doubt, that Charlie was right. I had a mission.

CHAPTER TWENTY-THREE

UNREASONABLE REQUESTS

I began to speak at prayer groups and churches, telling the story of my survival, renewed faith and my belief in Y'shua as the Messiah of Israel. These public appearances marked some of the first times I'd ever spoken of my family and the Holocaust. I was astounded at my confidence to speak and teach in front of people. After all, I hadn't been to school since I was eleven. I had to rely on God to give me the words to say.

As my speaking engagements became more frequent, my house became more crowded. As many as 22 kids sometimes slept wherever they could find a space. Our house was a sort of refuge for kids whose parents had reacted adversely to their faith in Y'shua. The word had gone out: "There's a place for you at the Price house." They were good kids, but it was becoming a bit unmanageable.

In the midst of all this, I noticed I was gaining a reputation. When neighbors walked past my house on their way to synagogue, they would turn away, just as I had turned away from the church in my neighborhood in Poland. Old friends ignored me on the street or in the supermarket. I was not only a pariah, I became invisible.

As for Charlie, he was a constant support to me. Soon after I started speaking in public, Charlie went in for another operation on both his knees. When Charlie told the doctor he'd been feeling weak and tired, the doctor advised him to move to a warmer climate, for instance Florida. He said that Charlie's health would improve in warmer weather.

I was torn. I'd finally fixed the house the way I liked it. I'd arranged the sewing and dining rooms and painted the whole house myself. My home was now my castle. But when the doctors insisted that by moving to a warmer climate, Charlie could live another ten years, I knew we had to go.

So in 1976 we moved to Florida. I convinced myself that we were only relocating for a short time. After settling in our new home, we found a Messianic congregation that was just starting up. But I was unhappy. Some mornings I would get up at 4:30 and sit alone on the porch in my rocking chair and cry. One morning, Charlie came out and saw me. He knew I was hurting.

"Okay, we'll pack up and go back to Philadelphia!" he said. It was the middle of winter, and I knew what the weather would do to him. I suddenly woke up from my own self-pity. "No, we won't. This is our home now and we're going to stay here." Once that was settled, I began to speak again in different places. In between, we would visit our children who now lived in Maryland. Our lives were falling into place.

One day Sid Roth, from Messianic Vision, came to see me. "Rose, there's an event taking place soon called Berlin for Jesus. It's a big conference held at Olympic Stadium and thousands of people are going. I think you should be one of the conference speakers. I gave the event planners your name and they'll be contacting you." He paused, waiting for me to respond.

"Is this a sick joke?" I said. "There's no way I'm going back to Germany." Sid urged me to pray about it. A few days later, someone from Berlin for Jesus called me and asked me if I would consider coming to the rally and giving a message on forgiveness.

"I can't speak of forgiveness," I said to Charlie. "Not after everything that was done to me and my family in that country."

I went to the leader of our congregation and told him what was being asked of me. "Everyone wants me to go— Sid, Charlie, my kids—but I don't think I can go and talk about forgiveness when I really don't forgive the Germans for what they did to me and to the people I loved."

"But Rose," he said, "Consider the other side for a moment. What if you do go? And what if you can forgive? Think of the healing that would begin to take place in you!"

I still couldn't imagine it. My anger and bitterness over my stolen childhood and the murder of my family were attached to me in a peculiar way. If I thought about our suffering my muscles tightened up and acid churned in my stomach. It was unpleasant, but familiar. It was my defense against the painful recollections.

In January, I received a letter from Volkhard Spitzer, a pastor in Berlin who was organizing "Berlin for Jesus," asking me personally to come. The rally was to take place in June. After much consideration, I tentatively agreed to go, but my heart was not in it. I still couldn't see it actually happening. I figured I could just back out at some point and at least people could say I tried.

The next six months were a battle. Every day I prayed, and every day I felt deep inside me that I should go to Germany, but I refused to give in to that instinct. "God of Abraham, Isaac and Jacob. You know what was done to me there. Please, don't make me go back. Anywhere but Germany, Lord. Please, anywhere else!"

Charlie promised me, "I'll be right by your side. I'll protect you." I loved him, but I still didn't want to go. Not only was I angry, I was also afraid. "Nothing bad will happen to you," my friends tried to assure me. "You have no idea what people are capable of!" I retorted.

Eventually, June came and I finally called Pan Am and arranged for a ticket. The next day I called and cancelled it.

That routine continued for several days. Finally, the day
before I was to leave I called the airline and they told me
that if I wanted a ticket I would have to come to the
terminal the next day and pay cash for it. "I think you must
have broken some sort of record for reserving and
cancelling," the salesperson joked.

Walking through the terminal to the plane was perhaps
the longest mile of my life. "Why am I doing this?" I kept
saying out loud and to myself. "I swore I'd never go back
there." Poor Charlie bore the brunt of my anxiety. "This is
your fault," I said to him as we found our seats on the aircraft.

We had four other people traveling with us, believers in
Jesus who had prayed for us and wanted to attend the event.
One of them was sitting next to a German passenger. He
turned and said something to her, but she couldn't
understand German and asked me to translate for her.

Since coming to America, I had refused to speak a word
of German or Polish. It was a gesture borne out of my
hatred for both the people who had hurt me and the people
who had permitted it.

I looked at this German passenger. Blond, sturdily built.
"He looks like a Nazi," I thought. But I prayed for God to
take away my prejudice. Then I was able to translate for my
friend. "He wants to know why we are going to Germany," I
told her. "I just told him where I will be speaking and he
says he will come hear me."

That exchange exhausted me and I sat back in my seat.
After the plane took off, and there was no turning back, I
figured I should actually determine what I was going to say
to the thousands of Germans who were coming to this rally.
I drew up an outline. "First I'll tell them what they did to
me, my family, my people. Then I'll ask them how they
could do such a thing." But I couldn't get past that point to
the forgiveness part.

As we began our descent into Frankfurt where we would
change planes for Berlin, my heart grew heavier and

heavier. When we landed, I forced myself out of my seat into the aisle and to the door of the plane. I didn't look out the window. When we disembarked, I froze. Charlie and the others didn't realize I wasn't with them and so for a moment, I was alone in the corridor. I stood there, rigid as other people maneuvered around me. My feet refused to move. Suddenly I was there again; the cattle car doors opening, the darkness, the selection upon arrival, the screaming as loved ones were separated from each other, the crematoria.

When my husband and the others realized I wasn't with them, they ran back to me. But terror had gripped my heart and they had to drag me down the corridor to a chair. A man came up to us and said he was a doctor. As soon as I heard those words in German, I snapped, "Get him away from me! I've had enough of German doctors! Don't let him touch me!"

But no words escaped my lips. I was screaming in silence. Finally I was able to shout: "Get away from me!"

My friends asked an airline agent if we could board the plane ahead of the other passengers. On board, someone gave me a drink and spoke to me in English. The memories receded, and I was not back in the camps, as I had been a moment before. The plane engines revved and we sped down the runway and took off like a bird for Berlin.

CHAPTER TWENTY-FOUR

THE EYE OF THE STORM

When we landed in Berlin, a young man ringing a bell and carrying a large sign reading ROSE PRICE was waiting for us at the gate. What a different reception from my previous arrival in Germany! He escorted Charlie and me into a waiting car, and as we pulled out, I yelled melodramatically to my friends, "If you never see me again, know that Germany finally killed me!"

We pulled up to the host hotel, one of Berlin's most grand. The lobby was a beehive of activity. Many well-known Christians were already there, among them Pat Boone and Pat Robertson with whom I'd appeared on the 700 Club. In that whirl of activity, I noticed Pastor Yongi Chou from Korea and Charles Duke. I recognized some Jewish believers, such as Sid Roth and Sandra Sheskin Brotman. I couldn't relax. The refrain that had worn out my mind for months: "Why am I doing this?" played over and over again, even as Charlie and I exchanged greetings with people.

We all felt united by a common purpose. In the capital of this country that to a large degree didn't know God before the war, and which sank into evil during it, we all wanted to see the people redeemed. That entire week the city seemed dedicated to our "Berlin for Jesus" campaign. Signs and flags floated everywhere. Dramatic performances were held at key points in the city. This center of power and business was being invited to turn to God.

One day, as Charlie and I were walking past a large church whose pastor we'd met, a group of young people resembling hippies of the sixties—mohawk haircuts dyed bright colors, extravagant clothing—was mouthing off at passersby. I was shocked at their behavior, perhaps because respect for one's elders was ingrained in Europeans during my youth.

"Who speaks English here?" I asked. They all did. I asked how they could insult others so easily.

"What do you know?" one of them, a spokesman for the others, remarked sarcastically. "Do you know what goes on in Germany today?"

"No, I'm a tourist."

"How can we respect our elders after what they did and now ignore? Read European history. We know what happened here."

Another jumped up and said angrily, "My grandfather was a Nazi! Do you know what that means? How can I respect him?"

Did I know anything about Nazis? I bit my tongue to keep silent about that. But a feeling of compassion for these youngsters blossomed in me. Each of these young Germans was outraged at what their fathers and grandfathers had done. They might be expressing it in a mode of dress and language confusing to the eye of an American, and offensive to the middle-class mores of modern Germany, but their hearts and ethics were in the right place. I couldn't tell them to respect their elders, but I knew—and told them—that respect was an essential ingredient of righteous anger. I invited them to Olympic Stadium on Sunday where I was speaking. My purpose for being in Berlin was becoming clearer.

Sunday came at last and we all went to Olympic Stadium, the great complex that Hitler built for the 1936 Olympics to serve as a showpiece for Teutonic superiority. It was here that an African-American, Jesse Owens, won six gold medals, piercing Hitler's theory of a German master race. And it was here, in 1981 on Reconciliation Day, the highpoint of the week, that a Jewish woman slated for extermination was to speak about love and reconciliation to about 37,000 Germans. I was seated up front on the platform along with the other speakers. Flanking me were two large Cops for Christ who'd asked permission to sit on either side of me.

At about 10:00 in the morning, the sky grew ominously black. I could smell storms in the air, and I started digging in my travel bag for my raincoat and umbrella. The stadium didn't have a roof. "Ask the stage manager to ground the mike just in case," I said to one of the cops next to me.

The rain held off. I listened as an Irishman spoke, urging unity among all peoples, particularly in Ireland and Northern Ireland. Then other men took turns speaking on reconciliation, and finally it was my turn.

I don't remember my name being called. I was suddenly aware that I was at the podium with thousands of upturned faces staring at me. I gripped my Bible and my notes.

I opened my mouth to tell those Germans what they'd done. Let me tell them of the "lagerarrest," the prison bunker where executions or floggings and other tortures were carried out routinely. Let me tell them of Dr. Rasher's Block 5, specializing in high pressure and exposure experiments, or Professor Shilling's experiments infecting prisoners with malaria. Let me tell them of the SS-Economic Administrative Main Office, an innocuous name for a bureau charged with ordering and overseeing the construction of gas chambers.

On the plane I'd scribbled an outline of what I would say. It was all here on a piece of paper. Yet I could not find the words to speak.

These German faces were spread out expectantly before me like poppies in a vast field waiting to be mowed down. And, yet thoughts of revenge boiled inside me: "If only I had a machine gun, I could wipe out at least the first three rows."

I turned to my friends in the front row. "I need you to pray for me," I said aloud. Charles Duke, the astronaut, and Pat Robertson came forward and stood next to me, and we prayed together in front of the crowd. My stomach was churning and my body was visibly shaking. I prayed, "God give me strength. Let me see you, not the Nazis." Then, as I looked out over the crowd I could swear I saw Hitler's face. I clapped my hand over my mouth and Pat Robertson continued to pray for me until I could look up again and the image was gone.

Then suddenly, a woman ran up the aisle toward me screaming and waving and pointing. A security guard grabbed her but she continued to shout and point.

And then everyone, the entire crowd, thousands of people were also shouting and waving and pointing in the same direction. They were on their feet, cheering and I turned to see what they were looking at.

They were pointing to my right where the large Olympic torch was burning. Beyond it, the American and Israeli flags fluttered in the wind. That Israeli flag was planted smack in the middle of Olympic Stadium where Hitler had proclaimed the thousand year Reich would be cleansed of Jews.

And beyond it in the sky I saw the most beautiful rainbow I'd ever seen. It was a double rainbow, and it intersected to form a cross. I have never seen anything like it before or since.

I knew then that God was there with me, and I knew that I could go on. I held the paper with my prepared remarks, but when I spoke, none of that came out. Instead, as I listened to my own voice, I heard words of compassion, not condemnation. It was like listening to someone else speak, and the message was one that only God could have given me.

Nothing in me wanted to forgive or forget what had happened to me. But I realized I *was* speaking of forgiveness and understanding. "Not you sitting here," I told them, "but another generation of Germans fell under a doctrine of hate and death. The German nation—the most educated and advanced in the world in medicine, science and art—became the world's worst murderer."

I looked down at this sea of faces, most much younger than I, and shared some of the things that had happened to me in the camps. Then I said, "But God's love is such that he forgives even all that. He forgives your country. He forgives you. And he loves you. He loves you so much that he was willing to be tortured and killed to prove it. And if he can forgive me in my rebellion and you in yours, then I can forgive you too. By his grace, I forgive you. I thank God that I'm here in this place, and I forgive you completely."

I sat down and bowed my head. I could hear the pastor at the podium crying. When he spoke he said, "Rose, Rose, look at the people!" I looked up and saw them all on their feet cheering. The pastor asked me to go back to the podium, but I couldn't. I raised my eyes to the heavens and spoke to my God. "I didn't want to do it, Lord, but once again, you sustained me."

But as it turned out, this had not been my last test. When I opened my eyes, I saw six men coming down the aisles, one by one. They approached the stage and said they were all ex-Nazis. They asked me to come down and to forgive them as I had from the podium.

This was one testing of my faith I had never imagined. I had just uttered words of forgiveness to thousands; it was far more difficult to stand face to face with one ex-Nazi and to forgive him.

Yet that is what I did. I climbed down the steps, not realizing what I was doing. I stood on the stadium floor and looked at the first man, and spoke words of forgiveness that I knew I could not have spoken the day before.

Another man approached me and said he used to be a guard at Dachau. He knelt in front of me and asked me to forgive him. Even then I was tempted to break his neck. "I could kill just one," I thought. But as my hands moved toward him, I heard myself say, "Did you ask Jesus to forgive you?"

"Yes," he answered.

I couldn't postpone his peace. I forgave him for what he had done to my family and me.

The rest of the day seemed a dream. The speakers and the music lasted well into the evening. Floodlights came on. I sat there between my two cops listening to others share their stories, letting myself be moved and healed, feeling bitterness evaporate in the same place where it had once rained down.

CHAPTER TWENTY-FIVE

REUNIONS

I returned to Florida and for the next year or so, I was invited many places to speak about forgiveness. I spoke at churches, meeting halls and schools. I loved talking to children, mostly high schoolers, telling them what had happened forty years earlier and how the word of God brought me out of a time of darkness into his wonderful light.

I had just returned from a shopping trip one afternoon when I got a phone call from my daughter Miriam. "Hi, honey," I said. "How are you?"

There was a pause on the other end of the line and then she said, "Mom, I found him."

I knew instantly who she was talking about—my son, Meyer. Ever since she was a teenager, she and her siblings had searched for the brother they'd never known.

I sat down, as Miriam explained that she'd found him quite by accident and convinced him to come to Florida for a visit. Upon hearing this, joy mixed in my breast with the pain of years of separation from my baby, my Meyer.

We mustered quite a welcoming committee at the airport—my sister, Sarah, her husband, Sam, my children, Charlie and I. In those days, passengers walked down a set of stairs rolled up to the plane. My dear Charlie, ever the "arranger," told the airline officials of the special situation, and they allowed us to go directly to the plane instead of waiting in the arrival area. I was right there when Meyer started down those steps.

Instinctively I knew it was him. And he, scanning the small crowd below, knew who I was. The moment he set foot on the tarmac, we rushed toward each other, embraced, and cried in one another's arms. "I'm your mother," I said, weeping. I couldn't hear or see anything else around us. Nothing mattered for the moment except that I had my child again.

Soon after that, as we were coming to know one another well, Meyer became deathly ill. He died a few years later. It is a horrible thing to lose a child, but at the same time, I am so thankful that I was reunited with him first.

Candy's marriage produced three wonderful children. We joyfully watched them grow. Their teenage years were easier on me than my own children's. My children sometimes still tease and argue with one another. This is my family. Every day I thanked God I survived so Charlie and I could create it.

Then, one day, Charlie had a heart attack, and was taken immediately to the hospital. The doctor said he needed a bypass. I'd never even heard of such an operation; they were new at the time. If Charlie didn't have the bypass, they said, he would be dead within a year. I was nervous, but after discussing it with Charlie, we agreed to proceed.

When they brought him out of the operating room, he looked terrible; his flesh was sort of a grayish yellow. They hooked him up to many different machines. His body couldn't do anything on its own. One machine breathed for him, one pumped his heart, one fed him and one gave him medicine. He remained asleep. Every day I tried to wake him and never could. The doctors said he would sleep for quite a while, but he was doing fine and would be home soon. I happened to look at his leg. They had removed enough veins to perform a quadruple bypass. I could see the pain in his face even as he slept.

After a few weeks, they transferred him from Intensive Care to a regular floor. He was awake for part of the day now, but the pain was more intense. The opening in his chest wasn't healing properly, and his body was riddled with arthritis. No medicine helped, no matter how high the dosage. The pain was constant. This man who never even took aspirin, who'd had a root canal once without any anesthesia, was now funneled painkillers around the clock.

I went to the hospital every morning and waited until he woke up. I would stay until past midnight, then go home, fall in bed, and come back the next morning. This continued for over a month.

One morning the nurse called me aside. "Your husband won't let me wash his body for him. He insists on taking a shower, but he can't do it alone. I volunteered to go into the shower with him, but he wouldn't hear of it."

I smiled, "I'll take care of him," I said.

I walked into his room. "Rosie," he said with a sweet smile. "Would you come into the shower stall with me?" So we stood together, my husband and I, under the pelting rain of the shower. I burst into tears when I saw all the incisions in his body. I held him close to me, supporting his now frail frame. Then I dried him off, powdered his body, and put some clean clothes on him. He itched terribly because the hair they shaved off for his surgery was starting to grow back. Between the itching and the chronic pain, the man was in misery.

At last the doctor said I could take him home. But the man I brought back to our house wasn't the same lively, humorous Charlie. He was very weak. I fed him 45 pills a day! I would line them up in a baking pan and separate them into piles. Some were for when he woke up, some for mid-morning, these in the early afternoon, these before dinner, and those before he went to bed. A kaleidoscope of colors sat in my baking pan. Tiny pills, large pills, capsules. He couldn't live without all the pills, yet they were killing him. The pain remained constant and took a greater and greater toll on him.

This went on for a few years. Yet he still encouraged me to keep up my ministry and accompanied me when I spoke locally.

In 1985, I received a phone call from Germany. Ari Ben Israel, a Jewish believer in Jesus who was actively preaching repentance and reconciliation in Germany, wanted me to come to Nuremberg for a reconciliation event.

I didn't want to leave Charlie. Ari apologized but he couldn't afford to pay for both of us, and because of the medical bills our finances didn't permit us to defray the costs.

"Go Rosie," Charlie said. "I want you to go."

On the plane, I said to my traveling companion, a German woman on the way to see her children, "I can't believe I'm going back to Germany again—and to Nuremberg of all places!" Ari, who I'd met briefly at the Berlin event, met me at the airport. On the way to the hotel, he told me a bit about himself. From then on, I felt as if I had another son.

The theme of the event was "Reconciliation and Understanding." Nuremberg strove to be reconciled with its past. The first day of the event began with a parade almost five miles long through the city; it was a silent march. There were no string bands or festooned dancers, only silent men, women, and children. I couldn't walk much due to things done to me at Bergen-Belsen. Ari got a car and driver to take me directly to the stadium.

I sat in the back of the car and looked out the window at all the people. Suddenly from around the corner came the biggest Israeli flag, I'd even seen. I started to cry. After all, Nuremberg was Hitler's favorite city. "What a wonderful God we serve!" I thought.

I sat there watching the parade pass by. People carried many large signs:

ISRAEL FORGIVE US FOR OUR ATROCITIES
THE CHURCH KEPT SILENT, BUT NOW WE ARE SPEAKING
WE BLESS JERUSALEM

I read those signs through tears. I could have sat there all day lost in thought, but I knew there was a certain urgency. We were going to Zeppelinplatze, where war pictures show Nazis goose-stepping past Hitler, standing maybe eight stories above them. When we reached the stadium, I got out of the car and approached the police escort and the driver. I offered my hand to the policeman, as is the custom in Germany.

"Are you the American speaker?" he asked. I acknowledged that I was. "Well, I want your autograph for my children. They're marching in the parade, and I wanted them to remember this day and who you are." I was happy to oblige. He handed me a program and I signed it.

I moved as fast as I could up the steps to the podium. It was moving, watching the parade coming from downtown to the stadium with the Israeli flag flying above it. I felt warm in my *kishkes*, my insides.

Music started up and speakers were called to the microphone. Sitting next to me was a woman named Paula, who told me of some of the horrible experiments that Dr. Mengele performed on her. I was overwhelmed and started to cry. I asked Ari to allow her to speak before me. I needed time to collect myself. Then I heard my name. As I walked to the podium, the stage manager came up to me, his face grave. "Mrs. Price, please don't look down at the floor."

So of course I looked down and saw the words cut in stone, "Sieg Heil." This was the exact spot where Hitler had stood, the manager explained. I wiped my feet on the words as I began to speak. My mind was filled with many thoughts, including what Paula had just told me. I only remember the words with which I ended: "God's love and forgiveness."

The weather, which had been threatening, now turned bad. A heavy shower of ice rain began to fall. Mixed with snow it created a chill cutting through even the heaviest clothing. I was still standing at the podium when Ari came over with a tall man beside him. "Rose, I want you to meet this man. He stood next to Hitler in this very spot. He was in charge of the Hitlerjugend, all the German youth organizations. He's become a believer in Jesus and renounced his Nazism."

My jaw dropped. The man looked down at me, got down on his knees where he and Hitler had stood, and asked me to forgive him in front of the entire stadium. It was as public a confession of sin as I have ever seen. Tears streamed down his face, as he begged for forgiveness. Just as in Berlin, I reached down, spoke words of mercy, and tried to raise him from his knee. When this Goliath stood and embraced me (and I am not a small woman), I was engulfed in his arms and chest. I could feel more parts of me being healed as we embraced. The rain stopped and the musicians came out to finish their concert.

The next day, I received an invitation to meet with Mother Basilea Schlink. I was extremely excited and honored. Weeks before coming to Nuremberg, I'd been given a book by her. Although she was not Jewish, she lived in Germany during the war, and had been continually harassed by the Nazis for her publicly expressed love for Jews. Her life was threatened daily, she was often called into Nazi headquarters, but she continued to teach that what the Nazis did was wrong and that Jesus was a Jew. Ari put me on a train to Darmstadt, somewhere between Nuremberg and Frankfurt. When I arrived, I was whisked into a waiting car, and I was off to Canaanland, a city within the city of Darmstadt. When I got out of the car inside the gates to the city, several sisters were there to meet me. They treated me as if I was the Queen of Sheba.

Their obvious love bathed me in healing balm. Yet these women were all German. That was a great revelation—these people too loved me *because* I was Jewish.

I was taken to my room and "ordered" to rest. I sat there drinking herbal tea, snacking on bread, cookies and cheese. Later that evening, I shared a quiet dinner with the sisters.

The next day after breakfast I was shown the grounds of Canaanland. Mother Basilea designed and developed Canaanland as a copy of Israel. Every mountain, all the highways and streets replicate the land of Canaan. We walked the grounds that day, praying at the Mount of Beatitudes and the Garden of Suffering. I learned that these women lived lives of constant prayer. Simplicity and prayer are their precepts; precepts I sometimes tend to forget. They grow all their own foods, some of which they give to the poor.

For three and a half days I walked, cried, and was cleansed. I was asked to minister in their church. And yet I still had not seen Mother Basilea. After three days, at lunch, I was told that Mother Basilea wanted to see me.

I was brought to a room and left alone. A door opened, and a sister led a small woman, quite thin and seemingly frail, into the room. She came and knelt down in front of me. I couldn't look at her face. It was literally glowing. She radiated calm and peace in a way I'd never seen.

"Rose, forgive me and my people for what we have done to you," she said softly. She was asking forgiveness because of her German ancestry. I looked at her and we embraced. "Mother, please forgive me," I said, "In my anger I have held your nation hostage."

If you don't forgive, you keep a person or a country in a cell. But you are in that same cell. If you forgive each other, as she and I did, then you are both set free.

I cried throughout our encounter. When I was once again calm, we went back into the dining room. "You know, Rose," Mother Basilea said, "Right after the war, during Christmas, several of the sisters and I sat down and wrote prayer requests. I prayed to meet a person who had gone through what you've gone through and yet could forgive our nation. Four years ago, I saw you speak at Olympic Stadium, and I knew that my prayer was going to be answered, even after all this time." She then pulled out the slip of paper on which she'd written her request to meet a survivor. I cried when I saw it, thinking how I almost didn't go to Berlin.

When it was time to leave Canaanland, I had mixed feelings. If Charlie had been with me, I would have stayed much longer to bask in the rest and love that fills that place.

The sisters who prayed for me then still do. I thank God for their love and I have visited them many times since.

During the following year, I did a lot of traveling for my ministry. In May of 1986, I returned to Maryland for meetings I was obligated to attend. Charlie wasn't feeling too well, and although I didn't want to go without him, he finally persuaded me.

His condition continued to deteriorate. Arthritis severely crippled his body. He developed a strain of glaucoma that left him almost totally blind. This was terrible for he was a voracious reader. He devoured newspapers, magazines and books. He even read the Help Wanted sections and the Obituaries. We had a sick joke between us: if he didn't see his name in the Obituaries, he'd know he was still alive.

I was in Maryland for almost a month and had a great time with my children and friends. I was asked to make an audio cassette containing one of my messages. It went smoothly, and my friend Terry drove me back to her place, where I was staying.

At the house, my friend, Barbara, was waiting for us. The phone rang and she asked me to answer it. It was Harvey, my congregation leader. The simple words he uttered turned my life upside down. "Rose, Charlie died."

"No! It's not true!" I gasped. I slammed the phone down with such force I hurt my hand. My children and friends were around me, comforting me, and gradually I calmed down. I called my son Norman, and told him to make arrangements for the funeral. Someone made me reservations for a flight home. I sat there numbly the whole flight back. I could not comprehend that Charlie would not be at home when I returned. At one point, I looked down and my blouse was soaked. I had been weeping and didn't realize it.

When I arrived in Florida, Norman was waiting for me.

"Don't say anything," I said. "It's not true. Daddy is going to come home. You'll see, by the time we get there, Daddy will be waiting." My mind flashed back to a time when I waited outside for my Poppa to come home. The same kind of desperation filled me now. I wanted so badly to believe what I was saying.

Norman held me. "Yes Mom, whatever you say." We got home at about 2:00 in the morning, but everyone was there waiting. Miriam had called all our friends. I walked by them all into the bedroom, changed my clothes, and went into the kitchen to cook something for Charlie. I knew he would be hungry when he got home. What was he doing out so late anyway?

"Your father's playing a joke," I said. "He promised he'd never leave me." I repeated over and over again that he would always be with me.

Denial is as powerful as grief sometimes. On the day of the funeral, I refused to get dressed. If I didn't get dressed, there could be no funeral and Charlie wouldn't be dead. My kids came into the room and forced me to get dressed.

When the limousine arrived to escort us to the funeral, I had to be forced to get in. I buried myself in a corner of the back seat. That is the last time I ever rode in a limousine. I will never ride in one again. At the memorial service, Harvey started the services but broke down, and Chuck took over. He also broke down, and finally Jack Zemstein finished the service.

When we got home from the funeral, my friends were there preparing to sit *shivah*. *Shivah* is a period of mourning during which the immediate family receives friends and relatives. Traditionally, and in Orthodox circles, a family sits *shivah* for up to seven days.

It was a difficult thing, to finally let Charlie go, and that's an understatement. I know that he was in agony during his last years and yet without him, I didn't know what would happen to me. Charlie was the one who made a human being out of me. When I met him I didn't know how to laugh or cry, or even what it meant to be a woman, really. I had forgotten completely how to love and be loved. It was

Charlie who had put up with all the things I went through. He held me through the nightmares, the yelling, the crying and the blaming. More than anyone else, he taught me how to trust.

Shortly after we finished sitting *shivah*, Miriam found me in my room. "Are you okay, Mom?"

I went to the closet and opened the door. Inside was a pale blue dress. "Do you remember when I wore this?" I asked Miriam. "Yes, on your anniversary," she said.

Since Charlie and I had eloped, I missed standing under the *chuppah*, the canopy at traditional Jewish weddings and watching Charlie break the glass. On our twenty-fifth anniversary we renewed our vows in a full marriage ceremony. I made my own gown for it. I finished it a week before the "wedding" day. Every time Charlie saw it hanging on the door, he would say, "Only you could have made such a beautiful dress, only you."

"He was so proud of you, Mom."

"I know," I said, looking at the dress, "He used to introduce me as his Proverbs 31. Sometimes people asked, 'Does she also have a name?'" Miriam laughed.

I closed my eyes for a minute, remembering how after the ceremony at the Temple, we went to Disney World for our "honeymoon." We were like a pair of kids. We rode every ride. I remembered screaming on Space Mountain, and promising after that I would never get on it again. We spent four glorious days there and returned every year. That's the Charlie I like to remember, the man who laughed all the time, who couldn't keep himself from telling jokes, and who had the courage to love me unabashedly, just as I was. I would marry him again in a heartbeat and take comfort in the fact that one day he will greet me again, after a long journey, at a different sort of homecoming.

CHAPTER TWENTY-SIX

AN UNFORESEEN JOURNEY

The days of mourning for Charlie passed, though I confess I still miss him sometimes. I became more and more involved in speaking to groups about forgiveness and reconciliation. I knew that Charlie would have wanted me to continue in this work.

In 1993, I attended a meeting at a private Swiss retreat. While we were there, the committee was planning an engagement in Hanover, Germany. A thought hit me, and I could not shake it. "Is Hanover far from Bergen-Belsen?" I asked. My friends looked at me curiously, but nobody said anything at first.

"How far away is it?" I asked again.

"About two hours driving time, more or less," someone replied.

My head was pounding, and from deep within my *kishkes* a voice boomed, "I must go there!"

My hostess looked into my eyes and said, "I'll go with you." Her husband wanted to go too. He had a car and would drive. Two others wanted to join us. Since we had obligations at our Swiss conference retreat, one of the young men suggested he drive allowing our host to stay behind and cover for us.

The next morning after breakfast, we all met quietly at one of the gates where the young man's car was already parked. Though our intention was to leave secretly, our plans had leaked out, and another woman insisted on joining us. And there we were, a group of people just heading off to visit Bergen-Belsen almost as if it were a day trip to the country, only none of us spoke for quite some time. Finally I broke the silence.

"When we get there," I said, "Just let me be, please. If I cry, please let me cry. If I scream, let me scream. If I just need to walk, let me walk." I didn't really know how I would react. As we drove along the autobahn, I felt choked. I couldn't breathe, and I was crying silently. We saw the small road sign, Bergen-Belsen. It was such an ordinary sign, like any road sign, without a hint that the words it carried spelled death for so many.

As we pulled into a parking lot that looked much like one in any state park, I recovered somewhat. I stopped crying and could breathe more easily. The woman who'd joined us at the last moment was overcome with emotion, so we left her in the lobby of the reception hall. I asked at the information desk if I could have a private tour.

The woman behind the desk eyed me. "Please," I said. Then her voice lowered and she whispered, "You were here, weren't you?"

Something in me didn't want to answer. I repeated, "Can I have a private tour or not?" in a Germanic, demanding voice. It could not be done now, she replied, because tours were arranged months in advance. "If I wanted to come months ago, I would have written you," I said. "But I didn't want to come here until today. And so here I am."

Then she said it again. "You were here, weren't you?" Her voice was tender and kind. Finally, I dropped my tough facade. I nodded my head, yes. She asked me to come into her office. I said I wasn't alone. She called to others there who surrounded us.

"Please," I said, "Just show me where the main gate was. I'll find my barracks on my own."

She accompanied us to the main gate. I looked to the right, then to the left. In front of me was about eighteen inches of bare land. She asked, "Do you know what that is?"

"No, something seems to be missing." She explained that the land was bare because of electric wires that had been on the fence. The land had been burned so badly nothing could grow there except thorns and thistles. I could feel them under my feet.

A large marker indicated the entrance to the camp. I hesitated and then walked by it. As my feet touched the earth beyond the sign I suddenly stepped back into the past. I ran behind a small tree planted near the walk, hoping it would hide me, and I began to cry.

My friends surrounded me and wept too. I must have stood there for fifteen minutes. Finally I stepped away from the tree and walked in the direction of the monuments where the barracks were. I began to pick up stones because I felt that Bergen-Belsen was one enormous cemetery. In the Jewish tradition you leave a stone at every grave you visit as a sign that you were there. Thousands of people had died at Bergen-Belsen, many while I was there. There could never be enough stones, I thought.

I walked to the monument that I believed marked my barrack. I remembered trees surrounding it, and as I read the inscription, I cried loudly. As if a wall had been put in front of me, I couldn't walk further. I started screaming, "Bergen-Belsen! You died but I am alive! Look at me! I'm here!"

But my sense of triumph faded as I thought of the others who were dead. I remembered the faces of those picked for death during roll call every morning, their expressions as they marched off, knowing exactly where they were headed. "Why couldn't they have survived with me? Why!" My words gushed forth without any bidding. People walking by stared at me.

In the midst of all this screaming, I started to pray. I couldn't believe it—I was praying for Germany's salvation. Then I stopped. "Lord, not here. Not in this cemetery. I can't. You're asking too much of me. I cannot pray for them here!"

I had been teaching on forgiveness since 1982, but I had to come to this place, at this time, to learn of true forgiveness. I heard what I can only think was the voice of God, telling me, "Here you will learn what it truly is to forgive."

My screaming subsided and I stopped praying. The nightmare ended, and I became conscious of my surroundings. A young man lay on the ground near me, crying bitterly. He had heard me praying. "How can you forgive us? How can you even use the word forgiveness after what we did to you?" I went over to him and lifted him and held him in my arms. "I can do it because God forgives us all, no matter what, if we trust in him. He went through such suffering for us; he understands our pain. It is because of what he has done for me that I can forgive."

It was getting late, and I asked if we could stop at the gravesites so I could say Kaddish, the mourner's prayer. Both my hosts spoke perfect Hebrew, and taking out their prayer books, they asked permission to say it with me. "Of course," I said. We walked from grave marker to grave marker, placing a stone on each monument and saying Kaddish as we walked.

I'd promised the woman at the office that I would stop by before we left, and give her one of my tapes on forgiveness. As we walked in, the office staff stared at me.

We sat down at a table, and the woman who escorted us asked me to write out my name. She passed the slip of paper to another man at the table who riffled through one of those bizarre records the Germans methodically kept. After a few moments he looked up and said, "She isn't on the list. She's one of them." I assumed he meant I was one of many with a deep feeling for Jewish suffering who had never been in the camps herself.

"What did they call you when you were here?" the woman asked. She wrote down my name as a child, and handed it to the man.

"Here she is!" he cried. "Look, here's her sister, and all the people from her town." I asked to see the list. There was my name, my sister's name, my auntie's name, and the date we were put on the train to Dachau. "What are those letters before my name?"

"They mean you were imprisoned because you were a political activist against the government."

"Would you mind repeating that," I said. And he did. And I thought of the eleven-year-old torn away from her family. "I think it's time to leave," I said to my traveling companions.

As we stepped outside, three busloads of young people were getting off to take the tour. An older woman leading the group announced, "Now, don't believe everything you hear here."

I walked over and grabbed her, wanting to literally shake the hell out of her. Her ignorance caused my blood to boil. I was holding her tightly by the shoulders.

Then I felt tremendous strength in me; a strength that could only come from the Lord. I let go of this woman and turned to the young people and said, "What this woman just told you is a lie. I was in this camp and could tell you about the hell I went through. But you know," I said, "that's not the end of the story . . ." The woman broke away from me and disappeared. The young people gathered around me and began asking questions.

I knew we had to get back to the conference so I said, "If you want your questions answered, come to the conference where I'll be speaking and I'll gladly answer them all."

Back in the car, someone started singing a prayer song, and we all joined in. Then one of the women asked me why I had needed to go back to Bergen-Belsen. I didn't know, I said, but I'd found reasons once there.

"You know," I said, "I thought I'd let go of it all. All the hate, all the bitterness and the pain. But I hadn't. There was still a kernel of unforgiveness that needed to be rooted out.

And I think I had to go back and face my memories in order to find that kernel and destroy it."

"And how do you feel?" she asked.

I looked out the window at the countryside rolling by in the dusk. I thought of my family and my friends and my husband and the life we'd shared. I thought of Joseph, in the Bible, who forgave his brothers even after they sold him into slavery. I thought of Jesus, who said, even as the people were killing him, "Forgive them; they don't know what they are doing." I thought of how I'd wrestled with him and yet how he'd brought me to this place; how even when I'd left him and denied him, he'd never forsaken me.

I thought for a moment and turned back to the woman and said, "Alive. I feel truly alive."

We drove on silently. The road stretched out before us. The darker it grew outside, the brighter the headlights shone, illuminating our path as they pierced the night.

AFTERWORD

BENDS IN THE ROAD

There are times when I sit outside my house in Florida, looking at the clouds. Suddenly in that cloud I will see an image of a person screaming in terror or perhaps the menacing face of a guard. It's just there for a moment, and then it vanishes. And I wonder in those moments if there are many things my mind won't let me remember. I know that as long as I live I will never be totally free from the pain I've experienced. But God's love is sometimes illuminated through pain. This has been a most difficult lesson to learn, but I'm so grateful to know it and to be able to share it with others.

In 1999, I returned with my lovely granddaughter to Poland. It was yet another time of testing, of re-discovering the infinite forgiveness God gives us and the forgiveness that we can extend to others in his name, in his strength.

I close this account with yet another unexpected turn in the road of my life. After Charlie died, I eventually learned to be content as a single person. My traveling and ministry opportunities took up much of my time anyway. I didn't really have a chance to be too lonely.

And then, about nineteen years after Charlie's death, I was at a Messianic Jewish conference in Florida. While I was there, two of my friends insisted that I meet this man named Jonathan. Try as I might to resist the idea of being married again, I eventually couldn't help it. We've been married for five years. God has truly blessed me; he sent me the best husband he could find. Thank you, Lord, for watching out for needs I didn't even know I had. And thank you, Jonathan, for all your help in making sure my story was told.

Other Books from Purple Pomegranate Productions

Purple Pomegranate Productions, the in-house publishing arm of Jews for Jesus, has a full line of Messianic books, and other materials including Holocaust-related books and DVDs available at store.jewsforjesus.org or write for a free catalogue to:

Purple Pomegranate Productions
c/o Jews for Jesus
60 Haight Street
San Francisco, California 94102
1-415-864-2600
jfj@jewsforjesus.org